Teen
Prostitution

Look for these and other books in the Lucent
Overview Series:

Teen Alcoholism
Teen Drug Abuse
Teen Pregnancy
Teen Prostitution
Teen Sexuality
Teen Suicide
Teen Violence

Teen Prostitution

by Ruth Dean and Melissa Thomson

TEEN ISSUES

LUCENT Overview Series

LUCENT *Overview Series*

Library of Congress Cataloging-in-Publication Data

Dean, Ruth, 1947–
    Teen prostitution / Ruth Dean and Melissa Thomson.
       p.   cm. — (Lucent overview series.   Teen issues)
    Includes bibliographical references and index.
    Summary: Presents an overview of the problem of teenage
prostitutes, including some of the causes and consequences of
this phenomenon and what can be done to prevent it.
    ISBN 1-56006-512-5   (alk. paper)
    1. Child prostitution—United States—Juvenile literature.
[1. Prostitution.]   I. Thomson, Melissa. II. Title. III. Series.
HQ144.D43   1998
306.74'5—dc21   97-27452
                                          CIP
                                          AC

Copyright © 1998 by Lucent Books, Inc.
P.O. Box 289011, San Diego, CA 92198-9011
Printed in the U.S.A.

Contents

Introduction

ALTHOUGH TEEN PROSTITUTES live in the same cities and towns as ordinary teenagers across the United States, their world is very different. They are here in our communities, and yet they are hidden from most people. They are kids, and yet the life they live separates them from most other kids and from normal teenage activities and concerns. They are criminals, but they are the victims of repeated crimes. They are family members, but most have not known a family's love and support. They have independence, but they do not have freedom. They are earning money, but they live in poverty. They are sexually active, but without intimacy. They have escaped one set of rules but are forced to obey other, harsher ones.

The world of prostitution is so separate from the ordinary world that most people rarely catch more than a glimpse of it. If they pause to wonder about a teen prostitute's life—to ask what it's really like, what would make a young person want to live like that, or what prostitution does to a teenager—they will not find many clues in the ordinary world. Even when the news tells of the death or the arrest of a young prostitute, it rarely explains anything about the world that young person lived in.

Looking behind the surface of that separate world is one way to see how teen prostitutes really live. Even from an early age, these kids often have a different and painful experience of the world. The steps they take to avoid being hurt in the ordinary world often lead them, unknowingly, into the separate world of prostitution. Exploring what

Teens who run away from home often do so to escape difficult family lives, only to then face the dangers of living on the street.

prostitution means to the kids who are involved in it helps show what has worked and what hasn't in helping teen prostitutes return to the ordinary world.

For some teens, prostitution is a kind of turned-around way of trying to get the financial support and love that they need, but that their families haven't been able to provide. Yet their families may cling to a respectable image that is not connected to the harsh realities their child must cope with on the street. Lacking parental support and love, these teens would have a very difficult time trying to cross back into the world where they grew up.

One girl explained the attitude of her parents toward her life as a prostitute:

> My family knows about it, but since I left home and have been supporting myself, I gets [*sic*] along better with them than when I lived there. My dad, he don't say nothin' about it. My mother says she wished I wasn't out there, but she will accept me back and I am still her daughter no matter what I did.[1]

This girl sees her prostitution as something she "did," not as a form of sexual exploitation. She perceives her parents' lives as better without her presence—a very profound loss, and a strong barrier to her ever returning to live under their care.

"She didn't really care"

Another teen prostitute's name was published in the crime reports of her hometown newspaper. In this very public way, she was labeled as a criminal. Yet her story reveals that she, also, lacked support from the most important person in the life of most children, her mother.

> Yeah, she read about it in the papers when I got arrested for prostitution. So I explained it to her and it just hurt her so bad, *she said*. But she didn't really care 'cause she was trying to find some way of getting rid of having to support me, so it didn't bother her all that much. She said it did, and carried on a scene, but it didn't bother her at all.[2]

Her mother's respectability does not include a sense of genuine caring for her daughter's welfare.

These teens, like too many other runaways and hustlers on the streets of America's cities, have moved into a life separated from everyday concerns and values. The stories told by these and many other street kids show how different their lives are from the lives of most American teenagers. While all teens share many of the same hopes and wishes, these teenagers face quite different worries and problems. Their stories are a window into the separate world of prostitution.

1

Teen Prostitution in the United States

PROSTITUTION OCCURS IN most countries of the world, and this has been true since ancient times. Throughout history, cultures have had different attitudes toward prostitution and the people involved in it. These differences can still be found today. In some countries, prostitution seems to be an accepted part of life. Prostitution is legal in these places and is conducted openly.

In other countries, prostitution is hidden because it is illegal. In these societies, it is considered shameful and unhealthy for men to buy the sexual services of a prostitute. The prostitutes are shamed and prosecuted as well, but the practice of selling sexual services still continues. Wherever prostitution occurs, it has a strong effect on those who are involved in it.

In the United States today, prostitution is definitely not an accepted part of life. A few people argue that prostitution should not be punished. They think of it as an exchange of money for sex between two adults. However, most Americans strongly oppose prostitution, and it is officially considered to be a crime in this country. Several counties in Nevada do allow prostitution, but even there it is legal only for adults. Yet prostitution occurs in every state of the United States. And in the United States as well as abroad, prostitution involves younger people as well as adults. In every city of this country, teenage girls and boys can be found working in "the life," as prostitution is sometimes called.

Understanding the statistics

Researchers have tried to determine how many teens are involved in prostitution, but complete information is not available. The country's official crime statistics, published every year by the FBI in a book called *Uniform Crime Reports,* do not reflect the true size of the problem. In 1995 only 1,033 people younger than eighteen were arrested for prostitution, but the FBI points out that this figure is not an accurate record of the total amount of teen prostitution. Instead, the FBI explains that the arrest record shows something about what the police are doing to stop this problem. Typically, cities have campaigns from time to time to reduce prostitution, but only a few of the adults and teens involved in prostitution are arrested in sweeps by a vice squad. Cathy Spatz Widom is a professor of criminal justice and psychology at the State University of New York at Albany who studies the records of arrests for prostitution.

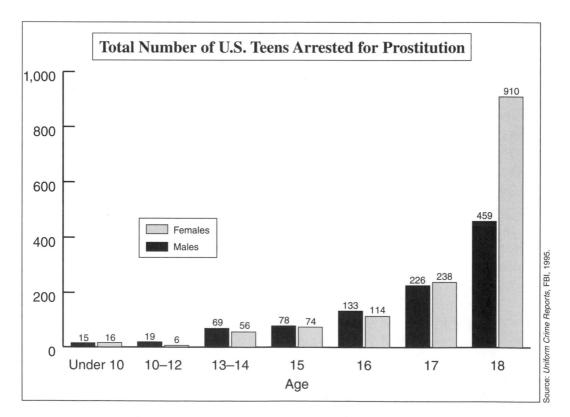

Total Number of U.S. Teens Arrested for Prostitution

Source: *Uniform Crime Reports,* FBI, 1995.

Widom says that the number of arrests is not a good measure of the size of the problem because most acts of prostitution do not lead to an arrest. She believes that far more juveniles are involved in prostitution than are ever arrested.

Another difficulty in making an accurate count of teen prostitutes is that people have found many different ways to sell sexual services for money. Some forms of prostitution can be disguised as legitimate businesses, and some criminals run secret houses, called brothels, where prostitutes work. These forms of prostitution are hidden from the police and other government officials, so no reliable statistics can be gathered about how many people are involved and how old they are. However, researchers like Diana Gray, a juvenile parole counselor in Seattle, believe that most of the teens who sell sexual services find their customers outdoors, on the street. That is why most of the studies of teen prostitutes focus on street kids.

Counting runaways

Some experts estimate the number of teens who are prostitutes by working with the statistics for runaways. Anyone under eighteen who is living on the street is officially considered to be a runaway, which is a crime in itself. The FBI reports that there were 181,562 arrests of runaways in 1995. However, even this official number does not give an accurate picture of the problem.

Statistics on runaways are discussed in a report written for the Office of Juvenile Justice and Delinquency Prevention, which is part of the U.S. Department of Justice. In this report, Gerald Hotaling and David Finkelhor review many different studies on the sexual exploitation of children. The studies show that most prostitutes begin as runaways. This is why establishing the number of runaways would be useful in showing the significance of the problem of teen prostitution. However, it is difficult to learn exactly how many teens are runaways. The Department of Justice report estimates that only one in every four or five runaways is ever arrested. On the other hand, some teens run away repeatedly and could therefore be arrested more than once.

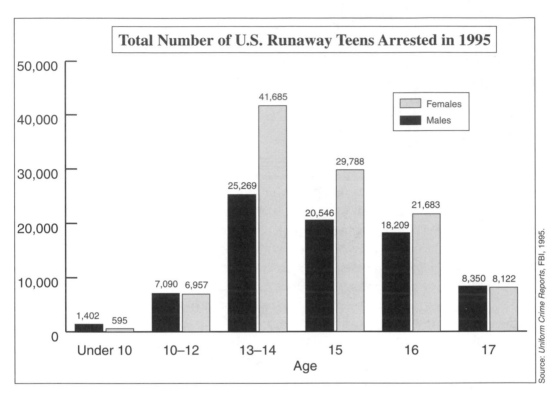

Total Number of U.S. Runaway Teens Arrested in 1995

Legend:
- Females
- Males

Age	Males	Females
Under 10	1,402	595
10–12	7,090	6,957
13–14	25,269	41,685
15	20,546	29,788
16	18,209	21,683
17	8,350	8,122

Source: *Uniform Crime Reports*, FBI, 1995.

The experts agree that estimating the number of runaway teens is the best way to measure the size of the teen prostitution problem in the United States. In addition, the connection between running away and entering prostitution is becoming clearer to the authorities. Researchers are interviewing street kids and learning about the forces that tend to push troubled runaway teens into prostitution. There is clearly a close connection between teens who run away from home and teens who enter prostitution once they find themselves on the streets of a strange city.

Estimating the size of the problem

Most teen prostitutes are probably never arrested. This is why the published crime statistics cannot tell how many teens are involved in prostitution today in the United States. Instead of using arrest records, most researchers study the problem and then try to develop an estimate of the real number. In 1988 Hotaling and Finkelhor summarized many previous studies and concluded that a million U.S. teens were running away from home or foster care each year.

Five years later, teen prostitution had increased, according to *Teen Prostitution,* a book written in 1992 for high school students by Joan Johnson. She is a high school teacher in Connecticut who has written several books about teen problems. Johnson gives a higher estimate for the number of runaways and also tells what proportion of these will become prostitutes. She writes, "Each year, between 1.2 million and 2 million teenagers hit the streets. Half will turn to prostitution to survive."[3]

Many runaway teens travel to a large city when they leave their home communities, and cities have their own estimates of the numbers of teens involved in street life. For example, the New York Peer AIDS Education Coalition believes that there are ten thousand to twenty thousand teenage hustlers, runaways, and prostitutes in that city alone.

These sources give different totals for the estimated number of runaways, as well as different percentages for the proportion of runaways likely to become prostitutes. While it is impossible to be sure of the exact numbers of teens involved in the hidden life of prostitution, researchers agree that hundreds of thousands of teenagers in the United States are involved today.

Illusions about life as a prostitute

Many people have seen a young person on a city street who might be a prostitute. However, few Americans have a realistic view of what life is like for teens like this, who are living by exchanging sex for food, shelter, money, or drugs. Prostitutes in TV shows and the movies often seem to be leading a glamorous existence. Their lives appear to be full of excitement and big spending. Sometimes teen prostitutes are portrayed in a different way, as middle-class kids who try living on the streets for kicks. These characters seem to have the ability to return to a safe suburban world whenever they choose.

Yet the counselors who try to help young people living on the street have learned that teen prostitution as it happens in real life is not a choice that can easily be undone. Diana Gray interviewed many teen prostitutes and found that they did not come from safe and happy homes. When they were growing up, they received little help or encouragement from their parents and were either treated harshly or ignored by their fathers. They had many reasons to be unhappy with life at home. These teens were attracted by the money they could earn as prostitutes. They were also curious about the fast life that prostitutes seem to lead.

Social worker Mimi Silbert and researcher Ayala Pines interviewed two hundred prostitutes to find out what had led them into prostitution. Silbert and Pines found that most of the prostitutes ran away from home when they were teenagers. Most left home to escape severe and repeated sexual abuse. These teens were not just making a lifestyle choice. Instead, they were reacting to very serious family problems. They did not have a safe, secure place where they could go if they wanted to leave life on the street. For too many young people like the teens that Silbert and Pines interviewed, becoming a prostitute is an act of desperation.

Dangers

Unfortunately, runaway teens often become victims of further abuse and exploitation once they are living on the street. Rape and assault are constant dangers. D. Kelly Weisberg, who has made a detailed study of adolescent prostitution, says, "A significant number of juveniles who have spent time on the streets have had frightening experiences with clients."[4] She discusses a study that found that most juvenile prostitutes have been abused or beaten by a customer. Although they are more often victims of crimes, some street teens admit to participating in violent crimes, such as assault and robbery.

Runaway teens who are escaping neglect and abuse at home continue to experience serious health problems in their new life on the street. The difficulties of street life

mean that almost all of these teens do not get the health care they need and suffer from malnutrition. They do not get decent food to eat and are likely to live on doughnuts, coffee, and fast food. They are more likely to get sick because malnutrition weakens their ability to fight infections.

If they become involved in prostitution, street kids face even more health risks. Because they are having sex with many strangers each night, they are in danger of getting sexually transmitted diseases, including infection with HIV, which leads to the incurable disease of AIDS. Some teen prostitutes think they can be safe from AIDS by not selling their bodies to men who are infected. They believe they can recognize a man with HIV by looking at him, but in fact this is impossible. Teens who have sex with strangers have no sure way of protecting themselves against this or other serious diseases. Additionally, many girl prostitutes become pregnant, and they do not get the health care they need for themselves or for the welfare of the baby.

Many teen prostitutes also abuse drugs and alcohol. These substances seem to make the life of a prostitute

Teen runaways can experience serious health problems living on the street due to malnutrition and exposure to harsh weather. Here, a teen wraps himself in a blanket to ward off the cold.

easier to bear, but addiction quickly endangers the young person's physical and mental health.

Being trapped

Teens who leave home and live on the street have no legal way to get the money they need for food and shelter. Laws designed to protect child workers mean that it is illegal to give a full-time job to someone under the age of eighteen. To get the money to survive, many begin selling sexual services and quickly become trapped in prostitution.

Diana Gray describes how teenage girls she has worked with saw prostitution as an easy way of making money: "Once the adolescent girl begins to prostitute, she finds herself entangled in a system which provides strong incentive to continue but limited outside contact."[5] This system limits their choices and their opportunities because prostitutes start to think of themselves as worthless. They give up hope for the future and just exist day to day. Street life makes it very difficult for teens to connect with anyone in the legitimate world who could help them find a better and safer way to live.

The role of the pimp

Runaways are also constantly in danger of arrest by the police simply for being an underage person on the street. Criminals sometimes offer young teen runaways a fake ID so they can pretend to be eighteen and avoid arrest. In exchange for the fake ID, many of these criminals demand that teens enter into prostitution. These men are called pimps. They draw people into prostitution and then live on the money that the prostitutes make from selling their bodies.

Teens are especially valuable to pimps because the pimps are well aware of a serious problem in American society. A significant number of adult men have not been able to form healthy sexual relationships with other adults. These men, called pedophiles, prefer to have sex with children. They are known to pay well for sexual services from the teens who are selling themselves on the street. This is why pimps are always on the lookout for young runaways.

Pimps know that pedophiles will pay more for sex with younger prostitutes.

Pimps are skilled at recognizing runaway teens who have come from a background of abuse and neglect. These teens do not have much self-respect, and they are eager for the affection and concern that the pimp seems to show for them. Gitta Sereny is a newspaper reporter whose detailed interviews with child prostitutes are recorded in her book *The Invisible Children.* Sereny writes, "The pimps know very well that what these lost youngsters primarily seek is a personal, human contact."[6] These teens have little sense of their own worth as human beings. In exchange for some attention and a sense of belonging, they are willing to accept the treatment they receive from the pimp and to endure the acts of prostitution they must go through with their customers.

The relationship between the teen prostitute and the pimp does not bring the real emotional support that these runaways are seeking. The pimp creates the illusion of love and caring between himself and the prostitute, but his goal is not to express love. His goal is to get the money that his teen prostitutes bring him each night. Pimps are known to rape or beat up their prostitutes so that they will obey him and continue selling themselves on the street to support him.

Instead of love, the lives of teen prostitutes are filled with even more abuse and exploitation than they endured as young children. As the abuse continues, hope for something better gradually fades away. The situation gets worse with time, and it becomes almost impossible for teen prostitutes to escape their dangerous lives. They seem to give up on themselves. Mimi Silbert says that teen prostitutes "retreat into a totally passive role in which they feel powerless, out of control of their life, debilitated, and psychologically paralyzed."[7]

Sexuality and growing up

Teens who are exploited as prostitutes lose many of the opportunities they need to become healthy, self-confident adults. All teens need self-respect, but this self-respect becomes more and more damaged by life on the street. Teens also must have chances to learn how to make good decisions about their developing sexuality. There are many different ways to achieve healthy sexual development, but it can happen only in relationships that are built on self-respect.

Instead of gaining self-respect, teen prostitutes have to deny their own needs for love and self-expression so that they can become what a stranger demands. They may have to pretend to enjoy sexual acts that they find disgusting or cruel. The lovelessness of sex on the street is in painful contrast to the genuine love that so many runaways have missed as they were growing up.

Trudee Able-Peterson's book *Children of the Evening* describes the despair and self-hatred of street kids. Able-Peterson worked with teen prostitutes in a crisis intervention center in New York's Times Square. She had been a prostitute herself but managed with great difficulty to escape "the life" and was working to help teens who were being abused on the street. Because of her background, Able-Peterson gained the confidence of some of the teens who came to the crisis center. As they got to know and trust her, they would tell her about their real feelings. She found that most of them had little self-respect and could no longer imagine any way to live except by prostitution.

The fast life

How is it that so many of America's young people abandon their homes and families for a life of danger and abuse? Most people cannot understand what would lead a teenager to take such a dangerous and even frightening path. Recently much has been learned about the reasons why teens run away and the forces that lead them into prostitution. Although teen prostitutes are technically criminals, punishing them has not been successful either in ending prostitution or in turning kids' lives around. Social workers believe that it is more effective to recognize that teen prostitutes are victims of crimes, often from their early childhood, and to provide help for them.

2

Entering into Teen Prostitution

TEENAGE GIRLS AND boys who are prostitutes almost never say that they planned to enter prostitution. Most of them report that they became prostitutes out of desperation, because they saw no other way of surviving. Each of these teens has a unique story of how he or she became so desperate. However, experts who have talked with many teen prostitutes have traced some similar experiences in their childhoods.

In a study of teenage prostitution among girls, Marjorie Brown writes,

> No one can say for certain that a particular background automatically breeds prostitution. However, studies of adult prostitutes reveal several common childhood experiences. . . . One or more of these conditions may occur in girls who became adolescent prostitutes.[8]

Teen prostitutes report that they came from troubled families, and many of them suffered abuse and neglect. Juvenile prostitutes often were very unhappy at school, and many suffered exploitation by adults close to them, including involvement in the production of child pornography.

While both boys and girls can be victims of neglect and abuse, some boys face another problem that can lead them to run away from home and turn to prostitution. Dr. Eli Coleman, a professor at the University of Minnesota School of Medicine, has interviewed many male prostitutes and written books and articles about their lives. He found that boys who enter prostitution are often escaping the conflicts that arose when their families learned that they might be gay.

Troubled families

Runaway teens almost all have one thing in common—growing up in a troubled family. They do not come from secure, encouraging backgrounds that can offer stability during the rebellious years of adolescence. Diana Gray says that the prostitutes she talked with

Most runaway teens come from troubled families that do not offer the stable and supportive environment teens need during the rebellious years of adolescence.

> tended to come from homes broken by separation or divorce and with many siblings. Home relationships in general were poor. Typical feelings are reflected by this statement by a runaway: "To be honest with you, there wasn't anything good about [home] because I had so many problems with my father. What he said went, and what I had to say wasn't important. What he said goes."[9]

The U.S. Department of Justice report says that many teen prostitutes come from broken homes:

A common theme in the literature [of research into teen prostitution] is that both male and female juvenile prostitutes grow up in homes broken by separation or divorce. This suggests that family problems are another factor contributing to juvenile prostitution. Research on juvenile female prostitutes suggests that from 66 to 90 percent grew up without one or both parents during part or all of their childhood. A higher than expected number of juvenile prostitutes have also spent time in foster/institutional care.

The report adds, "A stronger theme perhaps than even broken homes is the pervasiveness of poor family relationships during childhood and adolescence."[10] Family problems that have been experienced by many teen prostitutes include parental alcoholism, physical violence, hostility, rejection, a complete absence of parental involvement and guidance, and emotional abuse.

Lingering problems

Cathy Widom studied what happens to people who were abused during their childhood. She found that "in general, people who experience *any* type of maltreatment during childhood—whether sexual abuse, physical abuse, or neglect—are more likely than people who were not maltreated to be arrested later in life."[11] Troubled families lead to serious problems for many children as they grow up, even after they are adults and have left home.

Joan Johnson points out that families where children are neglected and abused are often struggling with enormous difficulties. "Sometimes one or both parents have problems with unemployment, alcohol or drug addictions, or other physical or psychological problems."[12] When troubled parents are not given the help they need, their children suffer. These kids are left with feelings of isolation, low self-esteem, and even the sense that they are responsible for their parents' troubles and their own lack of achievement.

This kind of background can cause children to grow up without the trusting relationships and the sense of security that they need. Brown says, "Girls from broken homes may perceive marriage more negatively than age-mates from stable families."[13] The girls Brown interviewed had sometimes seen their fathers hitting their mothers, and they did not develop a positive view of what marriage might be like. Instead, they thought of sexual relationships only as opportunities to get money. These attitudes can lead girls into prostitution.

Physical and emotional neglect

Many young prostitutes come from homes where there was little parental supervision or attention. Social workers call this problem "neglect." Diana Gray says that the girls she studied had poor relationships with their parents. These girls had too little supervision, and they lacked opportunities to talk with their parents about what really mattered to them.

> By the time these girls reach adolescence, parental ties and attachments to their family have become weak. Relationships with both mother and father are poor due to inadequate supervision, lack of intimacy in communication patterns, and consistent failure of the parents to provide positive social reinforcement in the form of attention, affection or effective communication.[14]

All children need attention and encouragement, but families are sometimes so troubled that they are unable to care for their kids. This neglect has far-reaching consequences as the children reach adolescence.

Marjorie Brown explains how the lack of attention and affection destroys teens' ability to form strong, trusting relationships. She says, "Without consistent affection, particularly at young ages, the child fails to develop trust; frustration, anxiety and aggression may be the result. As a teenager, the lack of trust may result in a sense of isolation from others and inability to form lasting relationships."[15] Brown describes many studies of teen prostitutes that show this emptiness in their lives. Teen prostitutes spend most of their time with people who have no emotional importance to them, and many of these kids have no friends at all. Childhood neglect results in lives without emotional support from other people.

Teens who long for attention and the family ties they have never felt can easily be drawn to people who seem to provide what they have missed. Pimps looking for young girls to lure into prostitution can recognize the girls who have been neglected. As a way of gaining their trust, pimps will often give these girls a lot of attention when they first meet them. One girl Gitta Sereny spoke to recalled how her pimp began to manipulate her: "He started to talk about marriage and about how much there is to learn, and he talked about life in general, and nobody had ever talked to me like that."[16] A man like this can quickly persuade a neglected teenager to work as a prostitute and to give all her money to him.

Physical abuse

Many teen prostitutes come from homes where they were repeatedly and severely beaten. The U.S. Department of Justice says that among teenage girl prostitutes, "severe physical punishment is extensive. Estimates vary that from

Physical and emotional neglect can have lasting effects on children as they reach adolescence.

50 to 70 percent of adolescents were physically abused by male and female caretakers. In many cases this abuse was quite severe and lasted long periods of time."[17] When Gitta Sereny interviewed juvenile prostitutes, she also found that they were victims of physical abuse at home. About half of the prostitutes told Sereny that they had been physically beaten by their parents or guardians since they were very small children.

Children who are abused are often taken from their abusive families, for their own protection, and placed in foster care. Many kids who end up as prostitutes were at one time in foster care or in a group home for troubled children. Most foster parents are compassionate and caring, and will do all they can to help the children in their care. However, the task is often very difficult. Many children and teens in foster care have experienced so much abuse and neglect that they are unable to trust adults and remain hostile to their foster parents. Sadly, some foster parents are themselves abusive, so the damage to the children in their care continues.

Some children are so severely abused that they die. For those who survive, physical abuse of this kind has a very harmful effect on the way that the children think about themselves. In *Violence and the Family,* Gilda Berger describes the mental and emotional damage to abused children: "Often, there is an inability to trust others, difficulties in getting along with both peers and adults, and general unhappiness. Many physically abused children see themselves as ugly, stupid, inept, clumsy, or in some way defective."[18]

Damaged spirits

In *Understanding Survivors of Abuse,* Jane Powers and Barbara Jaklitsch explain how abuse damages a child's spirit and causes behavior problems:

> Maltreated young people typically blame themselves for the abuse they have experienced. . . . Some tend to see themselves as responsible for everything bad that happens to them. This continuing distortion of reality contributes to low self-esteem, which can be immobilizing. Poor self-esteem both results from and contributes to a lack of success.[19]

KIDS WHO LIVE IN HELL

This analysis helps explain why teen prostitutes accept the many dangers they face on the street. They have been conditioned to believe that this painful life is all they deserve.

Sexual exploitation of teens on the street has been linked to sexual abuse experienced in childhood. Sexual abuse happens when a child is forced or persuaded by anyone to take part in sexual activity. Powers and Jaklitsch explain that sexual activity

> may include touching a young person for the purpose of sexual gratification or forcing a young person to touch an adult; exposing a young person to sexual activity, exhibitionism, or pornography; or permitting a young person to engage in sexual activity that is not developmentally appropriate.[20]

The abuser can be a relative of the victim or someone from outside the family. Sexual abuse by a family member is called incest.

There have been many studies on the effects of child sexual abuse, and on the connection between sexual abuse, running away from home, and entry into prostitution. The U.S. Department of Justice has reviewed a large number of these reports and offered three main conclusions: first, that many teen prostitutes were sexually abused during their childhood; second, that the rate of childhood sexual abuse is higher among teen prostitutes than among other teens; and third, that teen prostitutes experienced more sexual abuse than other runaways did.

Severe cases of abuse

The Department of Justice report also says that the childhood sexual abuse suffered by runaways and child prostitutes appears to be more severe than that suffered by other children. There are several types of sexual abuse that are considered particularly severe. One is abuse by a father or stepfather, which results in greater trauma than abuse by a more distant relative or by someone outside the family. Another is abuse that started at a very early age. The Department of Justice says that runaways suffer an unusually high rate of these severe types of abuse.

Many victims of sexual abuse run away from home to escape the brutality of their home situation. In her study of teen prostitution, Marjorie Brown says,

> Girls are frequently raped by alcoholic fathers, stepfathers, uncles or neighbors at a young age, and many girls become pregnant from the incestuous assault. The common response is to run away from the situation. However, once a child runs away from home, her parents may file a court petition, declaring her ungovernable and in need of supervision.[21]

Children returned by the authorities to such a home have little chance of escaping further abuse—unless they run away again.

Boy prostitutes also have suffered from sexual abuse as children. Eli Coleman, who has researched prostitution among adolescent boys for the Program in Human Sexuality at the University of Minnesota, says that many of them were physically or sexually abused as children. He discusses a study in which 25 percent of the male prostitutes reported that they had been sexually abused, and 10 percent of them said that this abuse had been committed by a family member. Even these figures, Coleman suggests, may be too low. "It is my clinical experience that many of these boys do not remember their early childhood abuse experiences, and that some do not become consciously aware of this trauma until they reach adulthood. There is a cultural taboo against admitting this kind of abuse."[22]

For many sexually abused teens, this maltreatment is not the only problem they face. As Widom points out, "Childhood sexual abuse often occurs in the context of multiproblem homes." She says that "the effects of other family characteristics, such as poverty, unemployment, parental alcoholism or drug problems, or other inadequate social and family functioning, cannot be easily disentangled from the specific effects of sexual abuse."[23]

Because of their sexual maltreatment, or because of a combination of circumstances, sexually abused children and teenagers suffer severe emotional and psychological damage. Their low self-esteem makes it impossible for many to escape abuse. Powers and Jaklitsch describe how some

Many teen prostitutes were sexually abused as children. Here, women in Boston express their outrage over child sexual abuse.

adolescents are so overwhelmed by the abuse they suffer that they stop struggling against it. They become withdrawn and lethargic or seem to try to be invisible. In *Outgrowing the Pain,* E. Gil explains that for many abused kids

> to comply [is] an important survival skill—Don't object, don't complain, just sit there and take it. They may also feel depressed and have a feeling of extreme deprivation. They may not have the interpersonal skills necessary to build or sustain satisfying relationships. They may be afraid to hope.[24]

Some abused children are so depressed and have so little hope that they commit suicide, perhaps seeing death as their only means of escape. Other victims of abuse escape the reality of what has been done to them by means of denial. This may be more common among victims of sexual abuse because our culture does not want to admit that such things can happen to children. Powers and Jaklitsch explain, "Denial is a natural response to painful experiences. Much of the escapist behavior in which these young people engage, including drugs, alcohol, constant listening to music, sexual activity, and aggression, enables them to deny their maltreatment."[25]

"You can't run away from your problems"

Other kids respond to abuse in a more active way—they run away from home in an attempt to escape. However, as one fifteen-year-old former runaway says, "You can't run away from your problems because it is just going to hurt you more in the long run."[26] Life on the street only brings more challenges and dangers.

It can be hard to understand how anyone would tolerate the life of a teen prostitute. Yet few outsiders understand the abusive histories of the young people they see offering sexual gratification to strangers for money. Gitta Sereny says, "The majority of girls who become child prostitutes appear to have suffered childhood traumas associated with early sexual experiences. This doesn't mean, of course, that any child who suffers such experiences necessarily becomes a runaway or a child prostitute."[27] But research does show that when children's sexuality is damaged and they suffer other family tensions or emotional stresses, there is a very good chance for serious problems to occur in the teen years.

Emotional abuse

Almost all other types of childhood abuse occur in combination with emotional abuse. Powers and Jaklitsch describe emotional abuse as consisting of "repeated threats of harm, a persistent lack of concern for a child's welfare, bizarre disciplinary measures, or continual demeaning or degrading of a child."[28] Children who are abused in this way begin to believe what is said of them and see themselves as worthless and stupid. The damage to their self-esteem can lead to serious consequences, including problems in behavior, failure in school, and emotional difficulties.

However, emotional abuse is often not recognized. Powers and Jaklitsch write:

> According to many service providers who work with maltreated adolescents, emotional maltreatment is one of the most common forms of abuse and neglect, yet it is rarely reported to CPS [child protective services] because it is so difficult to prove and is probably the least visible of all forms of maltreatment. . . . Some experts believe that emotional maltreatment is really the base for all other types of maltreatment.[79]

Yet emotional abuse is very difficult for social workers to discover. There are no simple signals or specific actions to identify. Emotional abuse often results from years of negative comments to the child and rejection of his or her need for love and affection.

Emotionally abusive parents and caretakers inflict severe pain on children. As a runaway explained to a *Time* magazine reporter: "Beating kids will hurt kids. Sexual abuse will hurt a kid. But verbal abuse is the worst. I've had all three. If you're not strong enough as a person, and they've been telling you this all your life, that you can never amount to anything, you are going to believe it."[30] This belief system can lock a teen into the degradation of prostitution.

Some social workers think that all the teen prostitutes who report having been physically or sexually abused should also be considered as victims of emotional abuse. Children who have suffered emotional abuse may also be unable to form positive relationships with adults and friendships with other kids. The poor self-concept that results makes them accept the sexual exploitation of prostitution that most teens would reject.

Difficulties in school

Children who experience neglect or abuse at home, or whose home life is unstable, often develop problems at school. It is hard for students who are fearful or angry to concentrate, and they often have discipline problems when their troubles cause them to "act out" in ways unacceptable to teachers and principals. Few schools have the resources to help troubled teens, and often the discipline they receive only increases their alienation from school.

Neglected and abused teens often have difficulty keeping up with the demands of school.

Brown notes that prostitutes generally have a low level of education and says, "Failure in the classroom compounds the increasing sense of isolation from traditional values. The teenager who has received little reinforcement

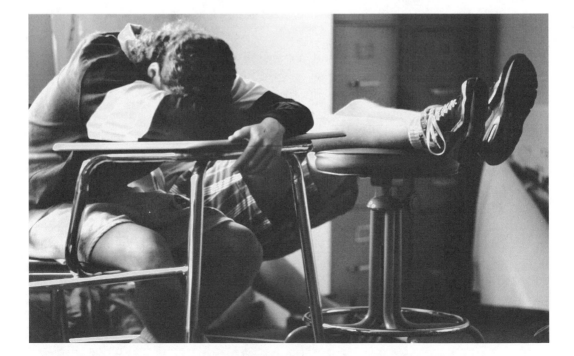

from the academic environment is unlikely to place much value on education."[31] These troubled teens have low expectations for their future. Neglected and abused children with academic difficulties are increasingly separated from the advantages that school is supposed to bring. They have less and less chance of taking their place in society as healthy adults.

Social problems at school can also damage a teen's chances of becoming a well-adjusted adult. Peers may call a classmate a "whore" to show that they think she is promiscuous, or sexually active with more than one person. It is very painful for a girl to hear this insult, whether she is really having sex or not. Girls who are labeled whores often do not fit in with a group of friends at school and may be humiliated in the neighborhood where they live as well. Marjorie Brown interviewed many girl prostitutes who had had this experience. She points out that a girl called "slut" or "whore" has a very hard time retaining her sense of self-respect. A girl who hears these humiliating insults may see herself "as rejected by mainstream culture for her sexual activity [and] may come to identify with, and thus see prostitution as a viable lifestyle."[32] Teens who reflect the strict attitudes of American society about a girl's sexuality may, without knowing it, be pushing her toward prostitution by tearing down her self-respect.

Rejection of gays

Another group of teens who may lose hope of being accepted and successful in our society are gay boys. Some of these boys become prostitutes, however, not all teenage boys who are involved in prostitution are homosexual. According to the U.S. Department of Justice, anywhere from 35 to 57 percent of male prostitutes describe themselves as gay, while 23 to 29 percent say that they are bisexual. This source reports that a boy who identifies himself as gay, or who is uncertain about his sexual orientation, can be "at higher risk of running away and getting involved in juvenile prostitution. Because he faces stigma and harassment from his family and community, a homosexual adolescent may run away."[33]

Because they often feel they are not accepted by society, gay teens are at a higher risk than other youths for running away and becoming involved in prostitution. This eighteen-year-old lives on the streets and makes his living by prostitution.

Many of the teenage boy prostitutes who have been interviewed by researchers describe abuse and family troubles. Coleman reports that in one study of 103 boys, most had highly traumatic family backgrounds that included broken homes, illegitimacy, rejection, alcoholism, brutality, inadequate schooling, and poverty. However, the rejection and abuse may arise from the boy's homosexuality. Coleman says that

> the homosexuality of many of the young male prostitutes precipitated many of the family problems and the decision to run away or to be thrown out. Unlike their female counterparts, who often flee their homes, the males were often thrown out because of their family's inability to accept their son's homosexuality.[34]

Some families respond to the discovery of a child's apparent homosexuality in a violent and abusive way.

What happens to runaways and throwaways

The effect of serious neglect and abuse at home is that teens may run away. Some runaways fear for their lives and see no other way to survive. Other teens—often called "throwaways"—are forced from their homes, or simply left behind when their parents move. Like abused runaways, these teens believe that they are worthless and lack the ability to develop personal relationships. When they hit the street, throwaways face the same problems that runaways face, along with the painful sense of having been abandoned to this life by those who should be caring for them.

Once runaways and throwaways are living on the street, survival continues to be a problem. Kids under the age of eighteen have no legal way of earning a living. As the San Francisco Task Force on Prostitution points out:

> Because of labor laws, established to "protect" those under the age of eighteen, most youth are not legally able to work more than part time. For young people who are living on their own and can legally work only part time at a job that pays minimum wage and offers little in terms of skill development and advancement, there are few opportunities for survival other than working in the underground economy, which includes sex work.[35]

Experts disagree on the percentage of runaways who eventually enter prostitution, but for too many abused children, sexual exploitation on the street follows a childhood of conflict and pain.

Pornography

An additional way that adults can exploit children is to use them in the production of child pornography. Some teen prostitutes report being asked to perform in pornographic movies or to pose for photographs. Studies vary on the importance of this form of abuse in leading children into prostitution, with some records showing that about one-quarter of the street kids have been involved. Child pornography is sometimes used to convince other kids to participate in a sexual act. Showing his victim a photo or video of this kind, the abuser will suggest that what he is asking the child to do is OK since other kids do it. The sexual exploitation of children—through pornography, neglect, and sexual abuse—is part of the cruelty that forces many children and teens into life on the street. There they are vulnerable to another form of exploitation: prostitution.

3

Life on the Street

EXPERTS ESTIMATE THAT about half of the teens who live on the street will turn to prostitution to survive. When they embark on life as prostitutes, these teens take a dangerous step, though few of them realize it right away. They are hoping to find a way of living away from abusive and neglectful families, and they often think that prostitution is a way of supporting themselves. However, they soon find that prostitution leads to even more abuse and exploitation.

An abusive and threatening pimp usually controls a girl prostitute's life and takes the money she earns. Only rarely do the boys seem to have pimps; nevertheless, researchers have found that, like the girls, boys do not retain their earnings for long. Boys on the street spend their money as soon as they earn it, and they have no friends except other street kids. As prostitutes, they are abused by strangers and neglected by much of society. Prostitution is a way of life that destroys their self-esteem as well as their health.

Physical dangers

Anyone living on the street faces serious problems, and being a prostitute makes these dangers worse. Kids who live on the street suffer from eating the wrong food. They eat what they can—mostly fast food—when they can. No one is available to prepare them healthful meals with fruits and vegetables, and they find it easier and faster to eat a snack in a café, when they can afford it. For all these reasons, teen prostitutes do not get the nutrition they need for their growing bodies. A poor diet can do long-lasting damage to the health of an adolescent even though he or she has reached adult height and appears to be full grown.

Street kids have to take what shelter they find, and they don't get the rest they need. Lack of sleep and lack of a good diet make them very likely to get infections. Because teens on the street are runaways, they live outside the law and do not want to go to hospitals or doctors' offices even when health services might be available for free. Some teen prostitutes get very serious illnesses, and others are in constant pain. Many street kids turn to alcohol and drugs, adding to their health problems and putting them in danger of becoming addicted. The money they earn is likely to be spent on drugs or alcohol rather than food and shelter.

Homeless teens also face the danger of street violence. They may be beaten or raped, and they are often too frightened to look for the health care they need after they are hurt in an attack.

Teen runaways sometimes turn to alcohol to cope with the difficulties of living on the street.

Special dangers for prostitutes

Homeless teens who turn to prostitution face all these dangers, and more. Every time a prostitute gets into a car or goes to a motel with a client, he or she could be attacked. Kids who live on the street often become victims of violence like beatings, robbery, and rape. One study of young prostitutes reports that 65 percent had been raped, and over 50 percent had been raped more than once.

These teens are also constantly exposed to sexually transmitted diseases. The most dangerous of these is HIV infection, which leads to AIDS. Practicing safe sex and using a condom can offer some protection from HIV, but teen prostitutes cannot insist that their customers wear condoms. They are in danger of angering a customer and face punishment by a pimp if they don't do what the customer demands. For most teens in this situation, the long-term risk of AIDS seems less important than the risk of being beaten up right now.

Teenage girls who work as prostitutes are at risk of getting pregnant. Weisberg's study found that "half of juvenile prostitutes have been pregnant at least once, a significant number have been pregnant more than once, and almost one-fifth have been pregnant more than twice. The average age at first pregnancy is 14.5."[36] Because of their illegal status as runaways and criminals, teen prostitutes rarely get the health care they need. And the way they are forced to live means that it is very difficult for them to take good care of a child.

A girl's story

Because they are so eager for the affection and support they never got at home, girl prostitutes are often drawn into a relationship with a pimp. At first he may seem to be offering protection and love, but soon this man "turns out" the girl he has befriended. A pimp who turns a girl out, in street language, is forcing her to begin selling her body to strangers and enter the life of prostitution.

Gitta Sereny interviewed a teen prostitute she called "Julie," who had been severely abused in her childhood,

Life on the street presents many dangers, including violence and exposure to disease.

both physically and emotionally. Julie said, "Finally I just couldn't stand it any more. So I went away." Julie went downtown, where she met a man.

> His name was Irving. I liked him, he said he'd take care of me. So I went to stay with him at this hotel, and he turned me out. Yes, I was real scared, but I figured it was better than home. You know, like I was feeling so bad about myself that I felt anything was better than that. Anyway, now I was just what my mother always said I was: a bitch and a whore.[37]

Julie's pimp told her what to expect from her customers, how they would approach her, and how she should ask them for payment. He also told her how much money she had to charge. Gitta Sereny asked Julie if her pimp told her what she had to do to get this money. Was she required to do whatever the customer wanted? Julie paused for a long time before quietly answering, "Yeah."

Turning tricks

Learning how to be a prostitute happens on the job. Most of the girls who have been interviewed about their experiences say that they just did what their customers, or "tricks," asked them to do. Diana Gray's study reports that most of the girls had never heard of the sexual acts that their customers demanded. Girl prostitutes become streetwise in other ways, too, like learning to watch out for the police vice squad, bargain with customers, and cope with the demands of their pimps.

One teen prostitute described to Diana Gray what she had learned from her pimp:

> He told me it was going to be rough and the police was heavy. And he told me when the cops come up and park, there's always a café there and you go in a café until they leave. But don't get caught in there. Like if you're just standing around jiving and there ain't no police and no vice out there, he's going to know you ain't out to make no money; you're just out to play.[38]

This girl learned to avoid the police on the one hand and her pimp on the other, but she had no protection against sexually transmitted diseases and pregnancy or against violence, rape, and exploitation by her customers.

How young prostitutes feel

Teens entering prostitution soon discover that they have escaped the painful problems they grew up with only to become caught in a life that brings them even worse difficulties. The glamour of "easy money" and the protection they seem to receive from their pimps cannot make up for the things they have to do to survive. The worst part of life on the street, though, is what prostitutes are paid to do: have sex with strangers. A fourteen-year-old girl explained her feelings this way: "The movies and television and books make you think it's glamorous. But you don't feel independent and wanted. You feel like a piece of hamburger meat—all chopped up and barely holding together."[39]

The relationship to the pimp

Studies have shown that almost all girl prostitutes are under the control of a pimp. Desperate for affection, young girls on the street seem to be easy for pimps to identify and manipulate. Lieutenant Bill Walsh, who works in the child exploitation unit of the Dallas police department, explains how girls become involved: "They don't know enough to fear people. Once they're in it, they realize that this person didn't have their best interests at heart."[40]

All the pimp is looking for is money. He recognizes that many of the customers for prostitutes are pedophiles, men who seek out sexual services from young teens. The pimp promises to give a teen runaway money, protection, companionship, and emotional closeness so that she will turn tricks for him. However, these are empty promises; they are only methods of manipulating girls into providing him with money.

Most of the girls Diana Gray spoke to handed all of the money they made each night over to their pimps. One way pimps control their girls is by letting them have only a very small amount of money at one time. In addition, pimps make many promises. The relationship between the pimp and the prostitute is based on fantasy. The pimp will claim that he is saving up to buy a house for them to live in when they are married, or a boutique for her to run. A teen prostitute interviewed by Gitta Sereny said that her pimp promised that he was putting some of her money aside in savings. "Now, of course, I know they all say that," the girl said. "It's the spiel, the method, the technique. Some are better at it than others. He was very good. I believed him."[41]

Money

Money has a powerful appeal for the kids who end up on the street. First of all, runaway kids need money to live on. But researchers who have talked to teen prostitutes have found other ways in which money is important to them. Most of these kids have such low self-esteem that they are surprised to find anyone willing to pay them for anything.

At first it can seem cool to get money so easily. Many teen prostitutes have described how clever they felt to be able to get money from adults. Some kids who grew up in troubled families and never had many opportunities have told researchers that they were glad to find out they had something they could sell. Marjorie Brown gives the example of an eighteen-year-old mother of two children who turned to prostitution:

> For the first time in my life, I had money to spend. I could show off my new clothes to my girlfriends. Some of them were already "working," and they always looked sharp. I got sick of stretching a $200 a month welfare check for me and my kids. It (money, clothes) makes me feel like somebody important.[42]

Before long these teenagers recognize that they are as powerless as they have ever been. What seemed at first to be easy money turns out to be a bad deal since young prostitutes do not hold on to the money they earn. Weisberg writes:

> Any earnings are expended quickly—on clothes, drugs and entertainment. In fact, the youth rarely have much money in their pockets. One researcher asked a group of young male prostitutes to count the money in their pockets at the time of the interview. More than half of the group had less than one dollar, and only seven boys possessed more than five dollars.[43]

Turning money over to pimps

For many teens living on the street, money seems to offer freedom. But when they turn to prostitution, money is often what their pimps use to control them. As Weisberg explains:

> One of the first lessons a young prostitute learns for her pimp is to turn over her earnings to him. Most juvenile prostitutes

are expected to turn over all their earnings to their pimps, and in most cases the pimp expects the prostitute to bring in a certain amount of money each day.[44]

Joan Johnson describes the case of Tracey, who was abused by her pimp. She made a lot of money for him, but he kept all of it, not even giving her the usual clothes and other things that pimps often buy their prostitutes. He often raped her and beat her, but Tracey continued to endure his mistreatment for some time. She says:

> Those people have a way of brainwashing you. There's no way of explaining it. I know now I could have walked away from it. But then it seemed so hopeless. He knew everyone. I knew he'd find me. And where was I going to go? Where was I going to live? I had nothing, no money.[45]

Abuse by pimps

In her interviews with teenage prostitutes, Diana Gray heard descriptions of pimps who were shockingly brutal. Yet many of these girls thought that it was right for their pimps to abuse them with words or by beating them. Some of the prostitutes even saw this violence as a part of their training, teaching them to hide their anger when a customer treated them badly.

Many teen prostitutes have been so psychologically damaged by child abuse that they see nothing wrong with being hurt by their pimp. They have learned to blame themselves for the abuse they suffer. Weisberg explains:

> Most prostitutes accept the violence as a way of life or feel they deserve it. Some are even flattered by it or accept it as evidence that the pimp cares for them. Many juveniles accept the abuse with passivity because they are convinced that violence is the acceptable standard by which men and women relate.[46]

Since they come from homes where violence is usual, many teen prostitutes seem to expect violence to be part of the relationship between a man and a woman. One of the girls Gray interviewed said, "We had our fights, like we were married—married people have fights. He beat me up a couple of times, but not very bad."[47]

Beth's story

Trudee Able-Peterson describes the painful, abusive life of a girl she calls "Beth," whom she met through her work with an agency that helps teen prostitutes.

Two days after Beth ran away she was broke. She could no longer pay the twenty dollars a night for her cheap, smelly room. Nobody would hire her. They didn't believe her when she said she was eighteen. She hung out at the Port Authority bus station for a few days, living on doughnuts and sodas. Then she didn't eat for two days. On the third day she was standing outside a restaurant on 43rd and Eighth, looking at

Many teen prostitutes feel trapped in a way of life from which there seems to be no escape.

the food and crying. That was when a tall, well-dressed man asked her if he could be of assistance to her.

When I met her, she had been working for him for two and a half years, on and off. She was sixteen and had been busted for prostitution exactly twenty-one times and beaten by her pimp fourteen times—one broken arm.

It was this abuse that drove Beth to seek help at the agency where Able-Peterson worked.

When I first met with Beth at the Center, she sat with her arms folded. I would notice in time that she always did that, as if she were still protecting her body from violation and abuse. She told me her story matter-of-factly, without emotion. . . .

"Do you miss him?" I asked about her pimp.

"I don't know. Used to him, I guess."

"How about when he beats you?"

I thought I saw her jaw clench a little, but she regained composure immediately.

"I just block it out. I don't feel it much."

Although Able-Peterson offered Beth every available support, Beth did not leave "the life" at this time. Later Able-Peterson saw her again on the street and recognized that she was still living in fear of her brutal pimp.

I saw Beth up the street just a few feet away. She was standing in front of the transient hotel on the corner. Our eyes met for a few seconds. I wanted so much to talk to her. But her eyes warned me not to even acknowledge her presence. Her pimp was undoubtedly in the bar across the street, watching everything she did.[48]

Boys in prostitution

Many boy prostitutes are runaways who need a way to support themselves. Sometimes another street kid will suggest prostitution as a way of making money for food and a place to stay. Sometimes a boy will be approached by a customer and find out about prostitution that way.

In a study of male prostitutes in the Times Square area of New York City, Robert P. McNamara describes how he saw a boy of about twelve walking through this area,

A transvestite prostitute waits for customers on a city street. Many young male prostitutes are runaways who turn to prostitution as a means of financial support.

which is known for sex shops and prostitution. The boy was approached by many men, some of them threatening, who clearly wanted to have sex with him. The boy that McNamara watched managed to escape. However, many runaway boys do enter prostitution because of threats from people like the men that McNamara described.

D. Kelly Weisberg tells the story of how a boy named Hal got into prostitution. He was seventeen when he moved away from home because of conflicts with his mother over his homosexuality. He reached downtown San Jose, California, where many of the people he met were prostitutes. One day when he was with his friends, a man approached him. "He offered me $25 if I would do his little thing with him. And I said 'sure.' That was the first one I ever did. I thought, 'That was great for 20 minutes of my time, to get that and then go party or something.'"[49]

Like the girls, though, boys soon find that the reality of prostitution is far from the "easy money" they were attracted to at first. "Matt" is the name Peter Axthelme gave to a teen he met on the streets of San Francisco. Matt's father physically abused his children, and Matt left home soon after being sexually abused by his parents' best friend. "There are some kids who can live just by stealing," Matt told Axthelme. "But here, well, I met this crazy dude with fuchsia mohawk hair, and he made the gay street life seem OK. Then he went to jail and I was on my own, and it wasn't OK."[50]

Donald Allen, a physician who studied male prostitution in Boston, writes about some young men who work only part-time as prostitutes and are still involved in legitimate activities such as school, college, or regular employment. Perhaps teens like these expect to be able to enjoy some excitement from prostitution without suffering any harm. However, many find that their lives are taken over by prostitution. Peter Axthelme spoke to a boy he calls "Wendell" who had that experience. This boy started out in prostitution with the idea it could be a part-time occupation that would bring in easy money. "I figured it would be fun to be a hustler," Wendell told Axthelme. "I'd seen guys in movies, living by their wits. I figured I could handle the sex part all right and stay in charge of things. It was OK, too, for one summer. I had tricks for money and a boyfriend for love."[51]

Soon, however, Wendell's relationship broke up. He had a regular job for a time, but when he lost that, he began to see how much trouble he was in. "I found out that I wasn't in charge of anything. The first time I *had* to hustle, I was as trapped as anyone out here. My life is ruined. And like the rest, I can't get out of the fast lane."[52] No statistics tell how many boy prostitutes succeed in escaping "the life" and how many end up like Wendell.

Street kinship

Other boys do fulfill at least one need through life on the street. The Department of Justice reports that some boys find in street life a sense of belonging that they never experienced as children in a neglectful or abusive home. This is a difference from the experience of girls who are prostitutes. Girl prostitutes lose their connection to others and live without friends. Boys seem to be more likely to feel part of a group.

As a young male prostitute told McNamara, "It's really like a family here. Everybody knows everybody else, everybody is basically friends with everybody else, and there's kind of a support group, you know. But it's like any big family of boys: you gonna have arguments and fight."[53] The sense of kinship is important, but it is not enough to replace the warmth and support that adolescents need from a real family.

Sonia Nazario wrote an article in the *Wall Street Journal* about a group of teenagers living under a busy highway in a dark, evil-smelling space that they call "the Hole." These teenagers get a feeling of kinship from their group, but it cannot make up for the abuse they have suffered or the violence of life on the street. As Nazario says,

Boys who live on the streets sometimes find a kinship with other street kids, which provides them with a sense of belonging they never experienced at home.

> After years of unhappy family life followed by the degradations of life on the streets, they think they don't deserve a better lot. "You are treated like scum by people," says Jennifer, now 17. . . .
>
> [Jennifer] recently awoke 60 miles from the Hole on a street corner, bruised and covered with blood after being clubbed

unconscious and raped by a prospective customer. "Your self-worth totally dies when you do stuff like that," she says.[54]

Violence by teen prostitutes

When teens lose their self-worth, they sometimes get caught up in committing acts of violence. In his study of young male prostitutes, Allen describes a group that uses prostitution as a way of assaulting, blackmailing, or stealing from homosexuals. Allen explains:

> [The members of] this group are mostly from the city, often housing projects, and they are part of a delinquent group also involved in other crimes. They are taught by older gang members how to be picked up by homosexuals and then threaten, assault, or blackmail the individual. They may threaten to report the homosexual to the police if he doesn't cooperate and will frequently beat him up even if he does.

One of these teens described how the group operates:

> When we see a guy by himself, driving slowly and looking at the kids on the corners as he goes by, Willy and I separate from the group. . . . [The customer] stops, opens the window, and asks if I want to go out. We argue on the price and settle. . . . As I open the door to get in Willy comes out of the shadows. . . . When he is finished I grab him and tell him to hand over his wallet and watch. We take all the bills he has, then jump him and beat . . . him.[55]

Violence on the street

Street teens are likely to be victims of violence, too. Both girls and boys who are involved in prostitution are likely to be mugged or assaulted. As Johnson points out:

> Thieves know that often they carry large sums of money, especially near the end of a night's work. They also know that prostitutes are reluctant to report a robbery to the police because they have no way to explain how they obtained the money in the first place and because prostitutes, as a group, avoid the police whenever possible. Thus, they are easy victims for muggers and drug addicts. They are also ready victims of rapists. They are on the streets late into the night in areas where crime is rampant. They are easily grabbed and dragged into alleys, where they can be raped and assaulted, often brutally.[56]

Teens who resort to prostitution generally lose their sense of self-worth and often suffer feelings of hopelessness.

Violence has tragic results for too many teenagers. According to Axthelme, the bodies of more than five thousand teenagers are found each year and buried in unmarked graves. These are street teens whose short lives have too often been marked by the sexual exploitation of prostitution.

Psychological damage and physical disease

Teenage prostitutes develop many dangerous techniques to try to protect themselves from the pain and disgust they feel when they have sex with strangers. Both boys and girls tend to separate their feelings so that they do not have to be aware of their own bodies and what is happening to them. They also avoid facing up to the dangers of their lives, especially AIDS.

Matt, one of the teens interviewed by Axthelme, tried to distance himself from what he was doing. As Matt explains:

> I created a separate personality for myself. With Johns [customers], my name is Michael, as in Michael Jackson. The tricks are sick for picking me up and I'm sick for doing it. But

by being a whole different person, I can keep from hating tricks so much. I swing my hips and think of Michael Jackson songs and I get through it.[57]

Matt could deal with his feelings this way, but he could not protect his body and had developed AIDS.

Some teen prostitutes know little about the dangers of HIV infection and AIDS, and some even believe that they can tell by looking at a possible customer whether or not he is HIV positive. Even those who know better cannot protect themselves, since, as Coleman says, the customers rarely give them the opportunity to engage in safer-sex practices. He says that most studies of these boys show that half of them have a venereal disease.

Teens who are living on the street as prostitutes are caught in a way of life that seems to have no escape. They have moved from a troubled past to a dangerous present filled with hunger, fear, and illness. They must break the law many times each day, and they have little hope that the future could bring them a better way to survive.

4

Prevention: Programs to Help Troubled Children and Teens

TEENS ENTER INTO prostitution for a number of reasons, and programs to deal with these problems can make a difference. Social workers are realizing that the best way to reduce teen prostitution is to help abused children before they run away from home and become committed to life on the street. Child welfare agencies are working to identify troubled families and provide support. Helping parents can prevent them from neglecting or abusing their children—the family background reported by almost all teen prostitutes.

Social workers, teachers, and family therapists are developing many ways to help children and their parents. One of the most important services needed by troubled families is substance abuse treatment. Counseling on sexuality can help prevent some children from being rejected by their families. When they receive help with school difficulties, children from troubled homes can get along better and begin to see their education as an opportunity for the future. Finally, improved treatment for pedophiles can reduce sexual abuse of children at home and later exploitation of runaway teens on the street.

Abusive homes

Many teen prostitutes grew up in abusive homes, and social workers have realized that dealing with family prob-

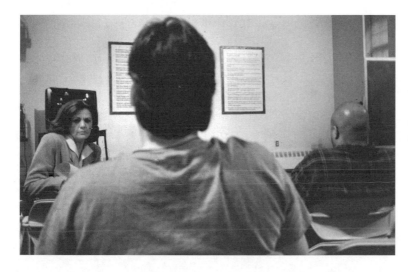

Teenagers attend substance-abuse counseling. Programs that help address problems such as drug abuse are one way to prevent teen prostitution.

lems can make life better for children and prevent them from running away. Programs to prevent child abuse have been developed in many areas of the country. One example is the Healthy Families project. In Maine it is sponsored by the Cumberland County Child Abuse and Neglect Council in the city of Portland. Sharon Bass describes this social program in an article in the *Maine Times* newspaper: "They train nurses, doctors, teachers, dentists and law enforcement officials on how to detect and prevent child abuse."[58] In addition, the project includes a voluntary abuse-prevention program.

Healthy families

The Healthy Families program serves all parents, not just abusive ones. Lucky Hollander, executive director of the Child Abuse Council, says, "We don't want you to have to be an abusive parent. We really try to target all parents, so parents get help before they hurt their children."[59] Hollander argues that keeping families from further involvement in abuse benefits the whole community. She describes the two most important factors in understanding and helping abused children: believing their stories of abuse and letting them know that people in the community are trying to make their lives better. It helps kids heal if they know that other adults care about their problems.

Many people in the community can work together to help both parents and children in troubled families.

The Healthy Families project is one result of the research and planning that has been conducted over the last two decades as Americans have realized how important it is to help children and parents in troubled families. Anne Donnelly is the director of the National Committee for Prevention of Child Abuse. She points out that "child abuse efforts throughout the world have increasingly focused on prevention, and these efforts have grown more sophisticated."[60] These sophisticated approaches are based on dealing with the real causes, not just giving young people simple advice about asking an adult for help.

Stopping child abuse is one of the keys to preventing teen prostitution. Here, a young boy sends a clear message to abusers.

Researchers have tried to learn why child abuse and neglect occurs. In an article, Donnelly lists many approaches
to the complex problem, including educating future parents about child development and the challenges they will
face in raising their children. Parents need help in coping
with stress, especially if they have special needs children,
and parents need medical care and social services as well.

Donnelly describes the many types of social services being provided to parents, especially one-on-one sessions between a parent and a counselor.

> Home health visitor-type programs . . . have been popular and
> have been shown to be effective, as have parenting groups,
> based either in hospitals or through various community set-
> tings, including schools. Some programs emphasize provid-
> ing parents with support (someone to talk to) and places to
> turn for help, while others stress parenting skills.[61]

Many programs focus on teen mothers and first-time parents, who often face more challenges in learning to take
good care of a child and, therefore, might be in danger of
becoming abusers.

Social programs have also been designed to provide assistance to children who might become victims of abuse.
Social workers and educators have tried to teach children
to protect themselves from the adults who might hurt them.
Early programs told children to say no and to tell an adult.
But social workers learned that children need more than
this simple advice. Interviews with teen prostitutes have
shown that they typically have little self-respect and often
believe they deserve any abuse and exploitation that they
experience. For this reason, recent child abuse prevention
efforts focus on helping kids develop self-esteem, learn
how to resolve conflicts, and establish healthy relationships with adults and with their peers. Children who have
these skills can often protect themselves from abuse.

Community efforts

In addition, the community as a whole is being drawn
into efforts to prevent abuse. Public service messages on
TV and radio have helped raise awareness of child abuse

issues and offered ways to help parents under stress. Donnelly lists some of these messages, from "It shouldn't hurt to be a child," to "We all have a role to play in preventing child abuse. If you know of a parent having trouble, reach out and offer some help."[62] Do these efforts make a difference? Different studies give different answers to this important question, but Donnelly presents statistics that reflect success. Between 1988 and 1991, when Donnelly completed her research, 15 percent fewer parents reported yelling and swearing at their children, and 13 percent fewer parents reported using hitting as a form of discipline. She writes, "These changes . . . provide tremendous hope for the longer term in preventing much of the child abuse problem."[63]

Children who do suffer from abuse at home need extensive help from social agencies, but these organizations often lack the resources to deal with increasing caseloads. In recent years, children's protective service agencies have had to focus on investigating abuse rather than on helping parents take better care of their children. At one time, an agency would have been able to provide help for the families that were identified as abusive. Today, however, the amount of reported child abuse has increased greatly, while funding for agencies has stayed at the same level. The result is that, across the country, children's protective service agencies are providing less family assistance, even as the problem of child abuse grows.

Substance abuse

A study by the Child Psychiatry Services department of Massachusetts General Hospital and the Boston Juvenile Court highlights some of the challenges that child protection agencies face in preventing abuse and neglect.

> The most serious cases of child maltreatment pose a number of difficult dilemmas for the court and protective agencies which deal with them. On the one hand, clinical experiences and previous research suggest that children who are left in severely mistreating homes have a 40–70% chance of being reinjured, and as much as a 5% chance of being killed. On the other hand, removal of the child from the parent—even a dan-

gerous, abusive parent—is itself traumatic for the child. In addition, removing the child can often lead to a series of "temporary" placements for extended periods of time. . . . Children in foster care are not necessarily safe from reinjury, and studies have documented the increased likelihood for children to be reabused while they are in "protective" care.[64]

After looking at the results of different ways to help abused children, the Boston researchers concluded that one type of family problem is the most dangerous to children. They found that substance abuse in the family led to the most serious cases of child abuse and neglect. When the abuse occurred, half of the parents were drinking heavily or intoxicated. The report concludes, "Substance abuse has been so clearly and consistently associated with child mistreatment that the Boston Juvenile Court, like other family courts, now accepts serious, untreated substance abuse as . . . evidence of parental inability to care for a child."[65]

Donnelly's study highlights this problem: "Prevention solutions to substance abuse as it impacts parenting are needed. Can we teach crack cocaine–addicted parents to parent? Can we stop substance-abusing parents from using substances so that they can parent?"[66] She reflects the deep concern that social workers feel about the harm a parent's substance abuse can cause to children under that person's care.

The Boston researchers also felt this concern. The families they studied had many problems, including poverty, lack of social supports, emotional problems, parental history of having been mistreated as a child, and inadequate education. However, substance abuse is one problem that they believe can be identified and treated successfully. These social scientists argue that dealing with substance abuse must be the first step in our efforts to help children suffering abuse and neglect at home.

Shelter for runaways

Some children respond to problems in their families by running away—by removing themselves from their home environments to risk the dangers of street life. In the past, police departments and social agencies have worked to return runaways to their parents. Arlene Stiffman, of the School of Social Work at Washington University in St. Louis, warns that this is not always the best solution, even if parents are willing to take a runaway back. She writes, "The homes of runaways are characterized by high levels of parent/child conflict, low levels of parental emotional support, and low parent/child empathy or positive regard. Significant numbers of runaways are victims of physical and/or sexual abuse."[67]

Sally Huncovsky, a Las Vegas probation officer, speaks with a young girl at a juvenile detention center. Huncovsky provides counseling as a means of discouraging girls from reentering prostitution.

Stiffman points out that agencies should consider whether parents' substance abuse problems mean that they cannot provide their children with a safe, healthy home. Mental health problems—including substance abuse, depression, and suicide attempts—occurred in a high percentage of the families of the runaways that Stiffman interviewed. She writes:

> Further, when treatment aims to reunite the child with his or her parents, service providers must be watchful for any indications of abuse, particularly in the presence of signs or runaway . . . reports of parental drug or alcohol abuse or antisocial personality. Unfortunately, at the present time there are few alternative placements available for youths, yet our findings point up the possibility that return to the family may mean entrapment in a situation fraught with mental illness, stressful events, and the possibility of abuse.[68]

She also notes that abused youth often need treatment for their own depression and substance abuse.

Sexuality

Counseling on issues relating to sexuality can reduce the family conflict that leads many runaways to leave home. For girls, early sexual activity can cause many problems. D. Kelly Weisberg reports that girls who later become teen prostitutes first had intercourse when they were only about twelve years old. Weisberg writes, "Sexual activity is often a factor in adolescents' family conflicts, and subsequent events, such as venereal disease, pregnancy, or abortion, contribute to family tension."[69] Families struggling to help a girl with one of these problems need a great deal of support and a range of social services. The prostitutes that Weisberg studied entered prostitution when they were fourteen, which is about two years after they had become sexually active.

Counseling services can also help parents avoid sexually abusing their children and protect children from abuse by other adults. Studies show that between one-third and two-thirds of teen prostitutes were sexually abused by someone in their families. Many social workers feel that this history of abuse leads children into early sexual activity and

Peer counselors speak with other teens during a therapy session. Teens who are coping with family problems can often find relief by talking to others about their struggles.

causes many additional problems throughout their lives. Counseling for parents, who sometimes also have a history of childhood sexual abuse, can break the chain and enable them to keep their own children safe.

Families of all types can find it challenging to help an adolescent who is rebelling against parental rules and expectations as a normal part of growing up. When rebellion includes sexual activity, the conflict between parent and child can be heightened. Parents of girls who act out sexually may find that their daughter is pregnant. Parents of some boys must deal with an even more explosive problem if their son is a homosexual, or simply not able to present a macho image. Strong cultural taboos against homosexuality may lead to serious conflict when a boy's bisexual or homosexual orientation becomes known to his family.

Sexual orientation

Dr. Eli Coleman has studied the relationship between entrance into prostitution and boys' sexual orientation. He points out that not all gay and bisexual adolescents become prostitutes. However, he also makes the point that homo-sexual prostitution mostly involves teenage boys. Under-standing the relationship between sexual orientation and prostitution is difficult for two reasons. First, Coleman's research has shown that a homosexual identity is not firmly established until a man has passed his adolescent years and is in his midtwenties. Second, someone who identifies himself as homosexual at one time in his life may not do so at another. Researchers cannot always tell whether a man is gay, or if he is, whether he always has been. This makes it hard for them to analyze the connection between being gay and becoming a prostitute.

Nevertheless, boys with a gay sexual orientation who later become prostitutes often report being rejected by their families. Coleman reports that the abuse these throw-aways have suffered at home leaves them with a feeling that they are worthless and can do nothing to make their lives better. Feelings like these lead them to become prosti-tutes and make it very hard for them to leave prostitution.

At risk

Coleman describes the services needed to prevent these disastrous results from harming gay and bisexual youths as they go through adolescence. He states that the teenage boys who are most at risk of entering prostitution are those who were abused as children and who are in a situation where they must find money to survive. "Prevention activi-ties must be directed toward these boys,"[70] he argues.

Coleman wants boys to be able to develop a strong self-image during childhood so that they can make good life decisions when they reach adolescence. Boys with a gay or bisexual orientation need ways to make friends and de-velop trusting relationships with other adolescents and with adults. "They need to learn how to develop positive conceptions of themselves and their sexual orientation,"[71] Coleman writes. He also wants social workers to offer ser-vices to the families of homosexual boys to reduce con-flicts within families over this issue. Helping families deal with homosexual children is one way to reduce the number of throwaway children, who are in great danger of entering prostitution to survive on the street.

School problems

Before they entered prostitution, many teens were having serious problems in school. Weisberg's research indicates that most teen prostitutes had given up on school before leaving home for life on the street. Only 19 percent of the teens in Silbert's study were enrolled in school, and many who were technically enrolled did not attend regularly. Most adolescent prostitutes never complete high school, with a surprising number dropping out after the eighth grade. These teens told researchers that they had totally negative feelings about school, had trouble getting along with other students and teachers, and didn't want to follow school rules. Some of the boys had trouble getting along at school because of their sexual orientation.

Not surprisingly, most teens who live on the streets have also dropped out of school.

Marjorie Brown also recognizes the difficulties that teen prostitutes have faced in school. She outlines changes that she believes would make a difference:

First, remedial education in public schools and correctional facilities must address the largely negative, punitive effect of prior educational experience. Teachers are needed who can impart academic skills without the endless drudgery and failure that create a school dropout to begin with.[72]

Brown adds that teens, especially teens from troubled families, also need sex education.

Joan Johnson says that it is important to help troubled students have a good experience in school.

In the long run, educational counseling and programs to aid a teenager in getting his or her high school equivalency certificate will not only give teenagers a sense of accomplishment and ensure that they have the basic literacy to function in society, but they will also open doors to jobs.

This type of education supports job training programs to give teens salable skills. Johnson adds, "Vocational training or the opportunity to go on to college will ensure that the jobs they eventually do find will pay enough to support them."[73]

Pedophiles

Preventing teen prostitution can also be aided by dealing with a serious problem, the role of pedophiles. These adults abuse children sexually while they are in the family and provide many of the customers for teen prostitutes on the street. Patrick Gannon is a therapist who works with adults who have survived childhood abuse. In his book *Soul Survivors* Gannon writes, "Most adults who abuse children have experienced some abuse of their own during childhood that was never treated. They are also survivors, although still in denial over what happened to them as children."[74] Gannon explains that therapists are still trying to learn more about the factors that would lead someone to sexually abuse a child.

One of these factors is called pedophilia. Abusers who were themselves sexually abused as children sometimes develop a sexual disorder as adults that directs their sexual preference toward children only. Treating such people, called pedophiles, is difficult, but it is very important, both for preventing sexual abuse of children and for reducing teen prostitution. According to Gannon, pedophiles often organize their lives "to gain access to new victims, despite the legal prohibitions against it. A pedophile may be a youth club leader, a teacher, a family friend, or a volunteer at a children's program, having the type of job or position that gives them contact with children."[75]

The search for an effective treatment for pedophilia continues. Given the harmful effect of this sexual disorder on children's lives, it is important to support research into effective programs and treatments. Daniel Campagna and Donald Poffenberger, in *The Sexual Trafficking in Children,* describe a series of approaches to treating pedophiles, but they also explain, "Pedophilia in its extreme forms cannot be cured, only treated."[76] Successful treatment requires that therapists help the pedophile completely restructure his sexual identity. Treatment approaches include psychotherapy, behavior modification, some kinds of medication, and putting the pedophile in jail while offering counseling.

Pornography

Many pedophiles buy and use pornographic books, magazines, and films that involve children in sexual activities. Joan Johnson says, "Worldwide, hundreds of thousands of children are exploited in this way to satisfy the sexual perversions of pedophiles and others who enjoy pornography."[77] The Office of Juvenile Justice and Delinquency Prevention has created a program called *Child Abuse and Exploitation: Investigative Techniques* to educate police officers and others who respond to reports of endangered children. The course materials explain that pedophiles use pornographic materials as they abuse their victims.

Sometimes parents exploit their own children in the production of pornographic photos and videos. Johnson points out that this is an abuse of a child's need for attention and love from his or her parents, and that the experience damages the child's ability to have a normal relationship with an adult. Johnson says, "For many children who are exploited by their own parents, pornography is a way of get-

A distraught woman holds a photo of a young girl who was murdered by a convicted pedophile. Finding an effective treatment for pedophilia may be one of the ways to prevent sexual abuse of children, teen prostitution, and unnecessary deaths.

ting the attention and 'love' all children desire. Their parents reward them with affection and treats and at the same time teach them that what they are doing is normal."[78] This form of abuse prepares children to enter prostitution by undermining their self-esteem and teaching them to provide sexual services to adults.

Breaking up the rings of adults who buy and sell pornography can limit the damage that this illegal trade inflicts on children. The *Child Abuse and Exploitation: Investigative Techniques* manual presents statistics on the size of this problem: "The sale of child pornography is estimated to be a multimillion dollar business involving an international network of pedophiles and purveyors of child pornography."[79] Although the link between prostitution and pornography has not been studied sufficiently, many teens who later entered prostitution have told researchers that they were involved in pornography as children.

The importance of prevention

Researchers have made much progress in identifying the factors that lead children into teen prostitution. Programs are being developed to help troubled families and to control some of the problems that endanger children. At the same time, funding for child protection agencies and schools has not kept pace with the growth in reports of child abuse. Yet all who work to help teen prostitutes agree that it is far more effective to prevent them from entering the life than to rescue them once they have been caught up in prostitution.

5

Programs to Help Teen Prostitutes

OVER THE YEARS Americans have taken many approaches to the problem of teen prostitution. Today, law enforcement officials and social welfare agencies are working to develop programs that provide troubled young people with the services and support they will need to break away from prostitution, which endangers both their bodies and their spirits. As Joan Johnson points out, "The best programs do not work in isolation. They are often a joint effort of social service work, the police, the courts, the schools, religious organizations and business."[80]

The first step is to find a place where street teens can be safe from pimps. Teen prostitutes need to be protected from the adults who exploit them sexually and abuse them physically to prevent them from leaving "the life." Then these teens need medical care and psychological counseling. Agencies have found that solving the problems of teen prostitutes requires far more than giving them a bed in a shelter and a hot meal. Only years of counseling and support can begin to repair the emotional damage these children have experienced.

Challenges to helping professionals

As a group, teen prostitutes are very difficult for social workers and counselors to assist. Most of these teens have had bad experiences with adults since they were small children, and they react by withdrawing, rebelling, and resisting rules. Children who have been abused do not find it easy to trust any adult, and they are especially wary of authority figures like police officers and teachers. As Johnson says, "When they enter treatment programs, these young people are easily bored, and they tend to be surly, manipulative, and angry. Most will have serious problems learning to live by the rules that any facility must maintain in order to be effective."[81]

A heartbreaking experience

In addition, counselors often find working with teen prostitutes to be a heartbreaking experience. It is very sad to watch a teen who desperately needs help return to the street—and to the exploitation that seems to be an accepted part of "the life." Trudee Able-Peterson's story of watching Beth go back to prostitution is an example of the sorrow that counselors often experience in trying to make a difference in a teen prostitute's life. The counselors that Joan Johnson interviewed told her how sad and frustrated they sometimes felt. Johnson comments:

Because teen prostitutes often have trouble trusting adults, many resist assistance from social workers and end up returning to the streets.

> As the counselors begin to build trust and honest communications with these young people, they will not find it easy to ignore their repulsion, shock, and indignation, the inevitable results of knowing teenage prostitutes well. These young people can be resentful and distressingly distant. They are almost always defensive. They have learned to be brutal and insensitive in order to survive the streets.[82]

In spite of these difficulties, outreach activities are the best way of reaching teen prostitutes and drawing them into programs that can help. Reaching out is necessary since teen prostitutes are reluctant to enter service programs on their own. Weisberg's report describes this challenge to solving the problem of teen prostitution:

Researchers and social service delivery staff constantly emphasize the difficulty of reaching the street population. These youth are fearful of any intervention, and they have learned to distrust adults. Many are afraid they will be sent home or jailed, and gay-identified youth often fear rejection by insensitive agency staff or physical assault by other, nongay youth.[83]

Street outreach workers devote many hours to gaining the trust of teen prostitutes so that they can offer them the help they need. But, as the outreach workers told Weisberg, they have the best success if they can reach a teen within one or two weeks of arrival on the street. Weisberg says, "The street worker may buy a youth coffee or donuts and sit and listen to the youth's problems, but only gradually will the youth trust the worker and ask for assistance."[84] Other teens turn to an outreach worker much later. A prostitute may ask for help when a very difficult problem occurs, like a drug overdose, the disappearance or killing of a friend, or being arrested.

Counseling

Programs to help teen prostitutes depend on the right kind of counseling. Mimi Silbert and Ayala Pines did research to help social workers plan programs that would be most effective for prostitutes. Silbert and Pines describe the best kind of counseling as "victim-oriented." This phrase means that the counselors should approach runaways and prostitutes as victims of long-term sexual exploitation, even though the teens may seem extremely tough and streetwise. Silbert explains, "The social worker who treats street prostitutes can assume they have a pattern of disturbed growth marked by physical, emotional, and sexual abuses and can help them share these experiences as a first step in therapy."[85]

Studies have shown that most teen prostitutes have suffered abuse and neglect. Sexual abuse by a close family member, or incest, has been shown to be the most damaging form of abuse. This background often makes it even harder for a street teen to accept the counseling that is desperately needed. E. Sue Blume, a therapist, has written about dealing with this challenge to counseling in a book called *Secret Survivors: Uncovering Incest and Its After-effects in Women.* Based on her experiences in helping incest survivors, Blume explains:

> Incest is possibly the most crippling experience that a child can endure. It is a violation of body, boundaries, and trust. Unless identified and dealt with, the emotional and behavioral aftereffects can stay with the victim. The very defenses that initially protect the incest survivor later lock these problems into place, interfering with adult functioning and preventing healing or change.[86]

As Blume's research shows, teen prostitutes who are also incest survivors can be very resistant to counseling.

Once a teen prostitute does take the first steps into counseling, the social worker needs to help with the feelings of despair and hopelessness that make it so hard to leave street life. Years of abuse beginning in childhood may have convinced the teen that he or she deserves punishment and can do nothing to achieve a better life. Silbert and Pines call this feeling "psychological paralysis," and say that it "underlies the inability of prostitutes to leave their self-destructive lifestyle. Before prostitutes can take advantage of behavioral or environmental changes, they must learn to develop a sense of control over their lives."[87]

Substance abuse treatment

Substance abuse counseling and treatment programs are an important part of the overall approach to reducing teen prostitution. Some teens already had a substance abuse problem before entering prostitution, but almost all use drugs or alcohol once they begin selling their bodies on the street. As is true with substance-abusing parents, teens must deal with this serious personal problem before they can benefit from other kinds of assistance.

Successful counseling also depends on the presence of strong, positive role models who can help teen prostitutes develop a new value system, according to Marjorie Brown. She says, "Teachers, correctional and probation officers, social workers and volunteers might well fill the void left by parental neglect."[88] Brown argues that one-to-one programs like Big Sisters can provide the consistent warmth and acceptance that help troubled teens recover from the emotional neglect they experienced in childhood.

Law enforcement

Police departments are usually expected by society to deal with the crime of prostitution. As Johnson points out, "Law enforcement with regard to prostitutes and prostitution is a measure of society's . . . commitment to ridding itself of this serious social problem."[89] Yet the police must respond to serious crimes like murder and robbery as well and often have little time available for working with street kids. Police officers find that a young prostitute who has been arrested in the morning may be back on the street that same day. Johnson interviewed a police officer who told her that he arrested one young girl four times on the same day. The juvenile court in that city had no program where she could be placed to keep her off the street.

Many researchers who study the teen prostitution problem recommend that law enforcement officials focus on arresting customers, since without people willing to pay for sex there would be no prostitution. Weisberg notes, "In reality, however, prosecutions of customers are all but nonexistent. The focus of law enforcement effort is the arrest of the prostitute, and few resources of local authorities are ever directed at the customer."[90] In recent years, teen prostitution is being viewed as sexual exploitation of children rather than as acts of juvenile delinquency. This change in attitude is helping agencies and governments focus on developing more effective ways to deal with the customers, who are the source of the teen prostitution problem.

The federal government

The federal government is helping teen prostitutes by trying to prosecute those who exploit them. In 1974 the federal government established the Office of Juvenile Justice and Delinquency Prevention (OJJDP) as part of the

Department of Justice. This agency provides national leadership and resources to prevent child victimization. The OJJDP develops programs that punish juvenile offenders, but it also provides treatment for juvenile delinquents, including teen prostitutes, and develops rehabilitation plans based on individual needs. Within OJJDP is the National Center for Missing and Exploited Children (NCMEC), which is a national resource center and clearinghouse of information on children who may be runaways endangered

A plainclothes police officer arrests a prostitute in Los Angeles. Many people view prostitutes as victims and believe officers should concentrate their efforts on arresting those who solicit prostitution.

on the streets. Since 1974 the NCMEC toll-free hot line has received over 905,000 calls requesting information or reporting a sighting of a lost child.

The Office for Victims of Crime is also part of the U.S. Justice Department. This government office helps agencies work together to deliver services to victims of crime. It is also the government's chief advocate for America's crime victims, who include the exploited children selling their bodies on the streets. This part of the Justice Department is helping law enforcement agencies change their approach so that more appropriate services can be made available to teen prostitutes.

The National Center for the Prosecution of Child Abuse helps professionals who are responsible for handling criminal child abuse cases. This organization works with police and prosecutors across the country to convict those who commit crimes relating to the sexual exploitation of children and teens. Historically, it has been difficult to prosecute

At the First World Conference on Child Prostitution, held in Sweden in 1996, a woman holds a banner that draws attention to the worldwide problem of child sexual exploitation.

pimps, who draw many runaway girls into prostitution and often use violence and threats to prevent them from escaping "the life." The National Center for State and Local Law Enforcement Training supports better prosecution by offering courses on how to investigate cases of child abuse and exploitation. The courses teach teams made up of law enforcement, prosecution, social service, and medical professionals how to manage a child exploitation case in the best interests of the teen victims.

Many studies have shown that teen prostitutes have a wide range of problems. The authorities must work together to provide all the kinds of help that they need. These local teams can include police officers, who otherwise have little ability to do more than arrest a teen, only to see the young person back out on the street within hours. Including prosecution attorneys helps make sure that the legal case against the adults who exploit teens is strong and that the right person receives the punishment in court. The social worker on the team helps find a safe place for the teen to stay and begins the counseling process. A doctor or nurse can provide the many kinds of health services that street teens need.

A Blueprint for Action

Staff members from the Office for Victims of Crime worked with the Education Development Center, Inc., and the Massachusetts Child Exploitation Network to develop a plan to guide agencies all over the country that investigate child pornography and prostitution cases and also provide services to the victims of these crimes. The plan is called *Child Sexual Exploitation: Improving Investigations and Protecting Victims—A Blueprint for Action.* The Blueprint is designed for criminal justice officials throughout the country who are concerned about protecting children and youth from sexual exploitation.

The Blueprint explains that child sexual exploitation cases, like those against pimps and people who use children to produce pornography, are hard for officials to prosecute. The laws are complicated to understand, and most prosecutors are not familiar with them. Typically, in a prosecution, the victim must testify against the person who has been accused of the crime. When the victim is an abused child or a teen who has been alienated from authority figures by life on the street, prosecutors need special skills to present the case.

Special support

The Blueprint explains that exploited children and teens have often been manipulated into the illegal sexual acts by someone like a parent or a pimp that they feel close to. "As a result, they may feel responsible for, or at least complicit in, the sexual behaviors. Young victims of pornography have lost control over images of themselves in print, on film, or in computer memories. These images may surface to haunt them at any time in their lives."[91] These children and teens need special support in dealing with police officers and lawyers.

Because teen prostitutes are often runaways, law officials from more than one state or city must work together to respond to their problems. The Blueprint says, "Lacking formal education or job skills, they survive by whatever means they can, which are often illegal. They may steal, sell drugs, or trade their bodies for a meal or a place to stay."[92] The result can be that law enforcement officials are the first authorities to deal with street hustlers, who could be seen as offenders, not victims. But officials need to treat them as people who have been victimized at home, hurt by a difficult life on the street, and exploited by a number of adults over a long period of time. Teen prostitutes are also likely to have AIDS and other serious health problems.

The Blueprint helps all the different kinds of agencies work together to provide medical, emotional, and legal support. The services include child protection agencies, victim assistance agencies, mental health centers, medical facilities, runaway shelters, drop-in centers, outreach projects, independent or transitional living programs, and youth services programs.

Criminal justice agencies need to draw on these sources for assistance to restore the physical and mental health of street teens. In addition, they will be better able to support the justice system in arresting and prosecuting those who sexually exploit children. All these types of support are necessary to stop teen prostitutes from continuing their destructive way of life on the street.

Runaway shelters

Runaway shelters are often the first place that a teen prostitute can find when he or she decides to seek help. The Blueprint says that almost 360 of these runaway programs are supported, in part, by federal grants. The two major goals of a runaway program are usually to "protect the youth from dangers 'on the street' (ultimately, by removing the youth to a more protected environment such as a shelter or foster home) and returning the youth to a place in mainstream society."[93] Teen prostitutes require intensive services, including counseling, drug treatment programs, and remedial and vocational education.

Social agencies have also developed a range of other ways to provide short-term help. The Blueprint lists emergency shelters, where teens can live for a few days, which are often connected to drop-in programs giving meals and counseling. In addition, "street outreach programs send youth workers to areas in which runaway and homeless youth congregate to offer services 'on the street.'"[94] Outreach workers try to find younger runaways and encourage them to go to a shelter. They also educate young prostitutes about the dangers of street life, including AIDS. Medical services are usually part of these programs and help teens suffering from poor nutrition, sexually transmitted diseases, and other health problems related to their lack of shelter and consistent medical care.

Long-term shelter

D. Kelly Weisberg reviewed many of the types of services available to teen prostitutes. She found a lack of programs that offer long-term placements for street teens who cannot return home. It is very challenging to develop successful programs for the most damaged teens, who have so many problems. Weisberg notes that these teens "are often destructive and failure-prone, and most programs working with street youth emphasize the importance of patience when dealing with this population."[95] Since the typical runaway shelter offers only immediate care, there is a great need for programs that can work with teens over several years. Therapy to address the teens' family backgrounds is important, and they need vocational training and job placement as well.

Teen prostitutes have many serious problems—legal, physical, and psychological. As law enforcement officials develop teams to work on child sexual exploitation cases, they also rely on the many agencies that offer programs aimed at helping street kids live a safer and happier life. Two of the most famous are Covenant House and Bridge Over Troubled Waters.

Covenant House

Covenant House is an example of the long-term shelter that Weisberg describes. In fact, Covenant House is America's largest shelter for homeless and runaway kids, and it does not place a limit on the length of time someone can live there. It has branches in New York City; Atlantic City and Newark, New Jersey; Washington, D.C.; Fort Lauderdale, Florida; New Orleans, Louisiana; Anchorage, Alaska; Hollywood, California; and Houston, Texas; as well as Toronto, Canada; Guatemala City, Guatemala; Tegucigalpa, Honduras; and Mexico City, Mexico. Almost forty-three thousand teens received services from a branch of Covenant House in 1995.

Covenant House offers the vocational training that is so important for teens who need a way to leave street life and support themselves in a legal way. Like many shelters for teen prostitutes, Covenant House also teaches independent living skills. These services are important because, as Weisberg points out, most street teens

> have not acquired the traits of punctuality, reliability, and good grooming, which are necessary if they are to obtain employment. Furthermore, once they find a job, these youth

*A billboard in New York
City advertises
Covenant House's
crisis hot line.*

have trouble developing a good rapport with supervisors, co-workers, and customers. They also must learn to budget and to perform such tasks as establishing a bank account and obtaining a driver's license.[96]

Bridge Over Troubled Waters

Another well-known shelter is Bridge Over Troubled Waters in Boston, Massachusetts. Bridge serves homeless and runaway youth by offering alternatives to street life and substance abuse dependency. This shelter has medical and dental services and provides education and job training. Counseling services focus on pregnancy and parenting. If it is impossible for a young person to return home, Bridge arranges for a different place to live.

The Bridge free medical van drives through the streets of Boston five nights a week so that volunteers can provide services to street kids. The van has a drop-in center, three fully equipped laboratories, and an X-ray room. The Bridge van offers counseling and nutrition and dermatology services. Doctors treat ear, nose, and throat infections; gastrointestinal problems; mild trauma; and sexually transmitted diseases. Testing is available for gonorrhea, strep throat, syphilis, pregnancy, and tuberculosis.

Attitudes toward teen prostitution

American society has taken many different attitudes toward teen prostitutes over the years. They have been ignored by people who do not want to think about the difficulties that street hustlers face every day. They have been made into characters that lead exciting lives in movies and TV shows. Yet on the streets of American cities, real teen prostitutes are selling their bodies for the sexual gratification of strangers. Some people label these teens "juvenile delinquents" and argue for strong punishments to prevent them from continuing to work the streets. Other people criticize teen prostitutes for choosing "the fast life" and urge them to stay at home, do their homework, and graduate from high school.

Researchers have learned that these approaches miss the real causes and effects of teen prostitution. Social workers and child protective agencies have developed many different programs to help troubled families and kids who are in danger of becoming runaways. To serve teens who have already entered prostitution, social service agencies are working together to help them build a better life.

Notes

Introduction

1. Quoted in Diana Gray, "Turning Out: A Study of Teenage Prostitution," *Urban Life and Culture,* January 1973, p. 419.
2. Quoted in Gray, "Turning Out: A Study of Teenage Prostitution," p. 419.

Chapter 1: Teen Prostitution in the United States

3. Joan J. Johnson, *Teen Prostitution.* New York: Watts, 1992, p. 57.
4. D. Kelly Weisberg, *Children of the Night: A Study of Adolescent Prostitution.* Lexington, MA: Lexington Books, 1985, p. 109.
5. Gray, "Turning Out: A Study of Teenage Prostitution," p. 423.
6. Gitta Sereny, *The Invisible Children.* New York: Knopf, 1985, p. 69.
7. Mimi H. Silbert and Ayala Pines, "Early Sexual Exploitation as an Influence in Prostitution," *Social Work,* July/August 1983, p. 288.

Chapter 2: Entering into Teen Prostitution

8. Marjorie E. Brown, "Teenage Prostitution," *Adolescence* 14, Winter 1979, p. 665.
9. Gray, "Turning Out: A Study of Teenage Prostitution," p. 405.
10. Gerald T. Hotaling and David Finkelhor, *The Sexual Exploitation of Missing Children: A Research Review.* Washington, DC: U.S. Department of Justice, Office of Juvenile Justice and Delinquency Prevention, October 1988, p. 16.

11. Cathy Spatz Widom, "Childhood Sexual Abuse and Its Criminal Consequences," *Society,* May/June 1996, p. 50.

12. Johnson, *Teen Prostitution,* p. 44.

13. Brown, "Teenage Prostitution," p. 671.

14. Gray, "Turning Out: A Study of Teenage Prostitution," p. 405.

15. Brown, "Teenage Prostitution," p. 666.

16. Quoted in Sereny, *The Invisible Children,* p. 15.

17. Hotaling and Finkelhor, *The Sexual Exploitation of Missing Children: A Research Review,* p. 17.

18. Gilda Berger, *Violence and the Family.* New York: Franklin Watts, 1990, p. 57.

19. Jane Levine Powers and Barbara Weiss Jaklitsch, *Understanding Survivors of Abuse: Stories of Homeless and Runaway Adolescents.* Lexington, MA: Lexington Books, 1989, p. 22.

20. Powers and Jaklitsch, *Understanding Survivors of Abuse,* pp. 12–13.

21. Brown, "Teenage Prostitution," p. 667.

22. Eli Coleman, "The Development of Male Prostitution Activity Among Gay and Bisexual Adolescents," *Journal of Homosexuality* 17, no. 1–2, 1989, p. 142.

23. Widom, "Childhood Sexual Abuse and Its Criminal Consequences," p. 48.

24. Quoted in Powers and Jaklitsch, *Understanding Survivors of Abuse,* p. 58.

25. Powers and Jaklitsch, *Understanding Survivors of Abuse,* p. 23.

26. Quoted in Powers and Jaklitsch, *Understanding Survivors of Abuse,* p. 145.

27. Sereny, *The Invisible Children,* p. 27.

28. Powers and Jaklitsch, *Understanding Survivors of Abuse,* p. 12.

29. Powers and Jaklitsch, *Understanding Survivors of Abuse,* p. 12.

30. Quoted in Nancy Gibbs, "Shameful Bequests to the Next Generation," *Time,* October 8, 1990, p. 42.

31. Brown, "Teenage Prostitution," p. 667.

32. Brown, "Teenage Prostitution," p. 673.
33. Hotaling and Finkelhor, *The Sexual Exploitation of Missing Children: A Research Review,* p. 15.
34. Coleman, "The Development of Male Prostitution Activity Among Gay and Bisexual Adolescents," p. 136.
35. San Francisco Task Force on Prostitution, *Final Report 1996,* http://www.ci.sf.ca.us/reports/sftfp/1tf.htm, p. 1.

Chapter 3: Life on the Street

36. Weisberg, *Children of the Night,* p. 114.
37. Quoted in Sereny, *The Invisible Children,* p. 34.
38. Quoted in Gray, "Turning Out: A Study of Teenage Prostitution," p. 413.
39. Quoted in Weisberg, *Children of the Night,* p.112.
40. Quoted in J. L. Hazelton, "Runaways Find Trouble in Streets," *Akron Beacon Journal,* March 26, 1997, p. A2.
41. Quoted in Sereny, *The Invisible Children,* p. 39.
42. Quoted in Brown, "Teenage Prostitution," p. 670.
43. Weisberg, *Children of the Night,* p. 164.
44. Weisberg, *Children of the Night,* p. 105.
45. Quoted in Johnson, *Teen Prostitution,* p. 86
46. Weisberg, *Children of the Night,* p. 109.
47. Quoted in Gray, "Turning Out: A Study of Teenage Prostitution," p. 416.
48. Trudee Able-Peterson, *Children of the Evening.* New York: Putnam, 1981, pp. 73–74.
49. Quoted in Weisberg, *Children of the Night,* p. 52.
50. Quoted in Pete Axthelme, "Somebody Else's Kids," *Newsweek,* April 25, 1988, pp. 66–67.
51. Quoted in Axthelme, "Somebody Else's Kids," p. 67.
52. Quoted in Axthelme, "Somebody Else's Kids," p. 67.
53. Quoted in Robert P. McNamara, *The Times Square Hustler: Male Prostitution in New York City.* Westport, CT: Praeger, 1994, p. 65.
54. Sonia Nazario, "Playing House: Troubled Teenagers Create a Fragile Family Beneath a Busy Street," *Wall Street Journal,* January 21, 1992, pp. A1, A12.

55. Donald M. Allen, "Young Male Prostitutes: A Psychosocial Study," *Archives of Social Behavior* 9, no. 5, 1980, p. 407.

56. Johnson, *Teenage Prostitution,* p. 133.

57. Quoted in Axthelme, "Somebody Else's Kids," pp. 65–66.

Chapter 4: Prevention: Programs to Help Troubled Children and Teens

58. Sharon Bass, "We Don't Want You to Have to Be an Abusive Parent," *Maine Times,* January 9, 1997, p. 3.

59. Quoted in Bass, "We Don't Want You to Have to Be an Abusive Parent," p. 3.

60. Anne Donnelly, "What We Have Learned About Prevention: What We Should Do About It," *Child Abuse and Neglect* 15, no. 1, 1991, p. 99.

61. Donnelly, "What We Have Learned About Prevention: What We Should Do About It," p. 100.

62. Donnelly, "What We Have Learned About Prevention: What We Should Do About It," p. 100.

63. Donnelly, "What We Have Learned About Prevention: What We Should Do About It," p. 104.

64. J. Michael Murphy, Michael Jellinek et al., "Substance Abuse and Serious Child Mistreatment: Prevalence, Risk, and Outcome in a Court Sample," *Child Abuse and Neglect* 15, 1991, p. 198.

65. Murphy, "Substance Abuse and Serious Child Mistreatment: Prevalence, Risk, and Outcome in a Court Sample," p. 198.

66. Donnelly, "What We Have Learned About Prevention: What We Should Do About It," p. 105.

67. Arlene Stiffman, "Physical and Sexual Abuse in Runaway Youths," *Child Abuse and Neglect* 13, 1989, p. 417.

68. Stiffman, "Physical and Sexual Abuse in Runaway Youths," p. 425.

69. Weisberg, *Children of the Night,* pp. 113–14.

70. Coleman, "The Development of Male Prostitution Activity Among Gay and Bisexual Adolescents," p. 147.

71. Coleman, "The Development of Male Prostitution Activity Among Gay and Bisexual Adolescents," p. 147.

72. Brown, "Teenage Prostitution," p. 676.

73. Johnson, *Teen Prostitution,* p. 161.

74. J. Patrick Gannon, *Soul Survivors: A New Beginning for Adults Abused as Children.* New York: Prentice Hall, 1989, p. 43.

75. Gannon, *Soul Survivors,* p. 44.

76. Daniel Campagna and Donald Poffenberger, *The Sexual Trafficking in Children: An Investigation of the Child Sex Trade.* Dover, MA: Auburn House, 1988, p. 45.

77. Johnson, *Teen Prostitution,* p. 91.

78. Johnson, *Teen Prostitution,* p. 91.

79. Office of Juvenile Justice and Delinquency Prevention, *Child Abuse and Exploitation: Investigative Techniques* manual, chapter 3, p. 81.

Chapter 5: Programs to Help Teen Prostitutes

80. Johnson, *Teen Prostitution,* p. 162.

81. Johnson, *Teen Prostitution,* p. 162.

82. Johnson, *Teen Prostitution,* p. 163.

83. Weisberg, *Children of the Night,* p. 242.

84. Weisberg, *Children of the Night,* p. 242.

85. Silbert and Pines, "Early Sexual Exploitation as an Influence in Prostitution," p. 288.

86. E. Sue Blume, *Secret Survivors: Uncovering Incest and Its Aftereffects in Women.* New York: Wiley, 1990, p. xiv.

87. Silbert and Pines, "Early Sexual Exploitation as an Influence in Prostitution," p. 288.

88. Brown, "Teenage Prostitution," p. 677.

89. Johnson, *Teen Prostitution,* p. 136.

90. Weisberg, *Children of the Night,* p. 213.

91. *Child Sexual Exploitation: Improving Investigations and Protecting Victims—A Blueprint for Action,* January 1995, http://www.ncjrs.org., p. 5.

92. *Child Sexual Exploitation,* p. 6.

93. *Child Sexual Exploitation,* p. 15.

94. *Child Sexual Exploitation,* p. 15.

95. Weisberg, *Children of the Night,* p. 244.

96. Weisberg, *Children of the Night,* p. 245.

Glossary

AIDS: A disease caused by a virus called HIV that attacks the body's immune system. AIDS is transmitted by sexual activity or by exchanging blood, such as when drug addicts share a needle.

child: In most states, anyone younger than eighteen.

childhood neglect: Failure of the family to provide a child with adequate food, clothing, shelter, or medical attention.

child pornography: Books, magazines, and films that involve children in sexual activities.

exploitation: Using another person for a selfish or immoral reason.

incest: Sexual activity between a child and an older family member.

pedophile: An adult who has a sexual attraction to children.

pedophilia: A sexual disorder that determines an adult's sexual preference for children only.

pimp: A person who makes money from the earnings of a prostitute.

prostitute: A person who exchanges sexual gratification for money, shelter, food, or drugs.

prostitution: The practice of selling sexual services.

runaway: A child under the age of eighteen who is away from home without permission.

sexual abuse: Forcing or persuading a child to take part in sexual activity.

throwaway: A child under the age of eighteen who has been forced to leave home or has been abandoned by his or her family.

Organizations to Contact

Several government agencies, including the two listed below, offer information on the exploitation of children. Most large cities have one or more shelters for street kids, and the addresses and phone numbers for some of the most well regarded are listed here. Hot-line numbers for information on runaway shelters, drug abuse, sexually transmitted diseases, and related topics can be found in the telephone directory.

Child Exploitation and Obscenity Section
U.S. Department of Justice
1001 G St. NW, Suite 310
Washington, DC 20530
(202) 514-5780

The Child Exploitation and Obscenity Section of the Department of Justice oversees the response of the federal government to child sexual abuse and exploitation. Prosecutors trained in this area can help officials who are prosecuting sexual abuse cases. The section also provides training.

National Center for Missing and Exploited Children
2101 Wilson Blvd., Suite 550
Arlington, VA 22210-3052
(703) 235-3900

The National Center for Missing and Exploited children gathers information that helps citizens and law enforcement agencies, distributes photographs of missing children, and provides information on effective state legislation to protect children. The center maintains a pornography Tipline to receive calls providing information that may assist an investigation.

A list of shelters in selected cities across the United States follows.

New York:

Covenant House
346 West 17th St.
New York, NY 10011-5002
1 (800) 999-9999

Provides crisis shelter twenty-four hours a day; offers long-range rehabilitation, community service centers, job training, and drug counseling in eleven cities in North and Latin America. Served over 42,000 teens in 1995.

Boston:

Bridge Over Troubled Waters
47 West St.
Boston, MA 02111
(617) 423-9575

Serves 4,000 teens a year. Mobile medical van provides basic health care to street kids and tests for pregnancy and sexually transmitted diseases. GED and job readiness programs.

San Francisco:

Central City Hospitality House
290 Turk St.
San Francisco, CA 94102
(415) 749-2181

Serves 1,500 teens a year. As part of their therapy, teen clients learn painting and ceramics, sell their work, and keep 60 percent of the profit.

Seattle:

Denny Place
210 Dexter Ave.
North Seattle, WA 98109
(206) 328-5693

The only licensed overnight shelter for kids under seventeen in Seattle.

Columbus, Ohio:
Huckleberry House
1421 Hamlet St.
Columbus, OH 43201
(614) 294-8097

Serves 900 teens a year. Emphasizes family support.
Staff go into teens' homes to mediate conflicts with parents, help with homework, or get dinner on the table.

Chicago:
The Night Ministry
1218 West Addison
Chicago, IL 60613
(312) 935-8300

Serves 6,000 teens a year. A bus goes out six nights a
week to provide on-the-spot health care and counseling,
as well as treatment and education referrals.

Nashville:
Oasis Center
1221 16th Ave. South
Nashville, TN 37212
(615) 327-4455

Serves 4,100 teens a year. A peer-educator program
trains teens, some of them former clients, to answer the
crisis line, lead prevention and education groups, and
serve on the agency's board of directors.

Washington, D.C.:
Sasha Bruce Youthwork, Inc.
741 Eighth St. SE
Washington, DC 20003
(202) 675-9340

Serves about 10,000 teens a year. One of its six shelters
is for homeless teen mothers. Girls attend public school
or prepare for their GED and learn parenting skills while
staff members care for their babies.

Pittsburgh:

The Whale's Tale

250 Shady Ave.
Pittsburgh, PA 15206
(412) 661-1800

Served 37,000 youth and their families 1995. In the Bridge Housing program, former runaways and homeless teens who have achieved certain goals live in a group house under minimum supervision. All hold jobs or go to school.

Suggestions for Further Reading

Pete Axthelme, "Somebody Else's Kids," *Newsweek,* April 25, 1988.

Judith Berck, *No Place to Be: Voices of Homeless Children.* Boston: Houghton Mifflin, 1992.

Gilda Berger, *Violence and the Family.* New York: Franklin Watts, 1990.

Suzanne Coil, *The Poor in America.* Englewood Cliffs, NJ: Julian Messner, 1989.

Nancy Gibbs, "Shameful Bequests to the Next Generation," *Time,* October 8, 1990.

Mark Stuart Gill, "Night Stalker: Hitting the Streets in the Name of Corporate Philanthropy," *Business Month,* June 1990.

Joan J. Johnson, *Teen Prostitution.* New York: Watts, 1992.

Jonathan Mandell, "House of Hope," *Good Housekeeping,* December 1, 1996.

Mary Rose McGeady, *Are You There, God?* New York: Covenant House, 1996.

Jane Levine Powers and Barbara Weiss Jaklitsch, *Understanding Survivors of Abuse: Stories of Homeless and Runaway Adolescents.* Lexington, MA: Lexington Books, 1989.

Lois Stavsky and I. E. Mozeson, *The Place I Call Home: Voices and Faces of Homeless Teens.* New York: Shapolsky Publishers, 1990.

Additional Works Consulted

Trudee Able-Peterson, *Children of the Evening*. New York: Putnam, 1981.

Donald M. Allen, "Young Male Prostitutes: A Psychosocial Study," *Archives of Sexual Behavior* 9, no. 5, 1980.

Sharon Bass, "We Don't Want You to Have to Be an Abusive Parent," *Maine Times,* January 9, 1997.

Shay Bilchik, "An Introduction to the Office of Juvenile Justice and Delinquency Prevention," Fact Sheet #43, July 1996, http://www.ncjrs.org.

E. Sue Blume, *Secret Survivors: Uncovering Incest and Its Aftereffects in Women.* New York: Wiley, 1990.

Bridge Over Troubled Waters, http://www.harvardradcliffe.edu.

Marjorie E. Brown, "Teenage Prostitution," *Adolescence* 14, Winter 1979.

Daniel Campagna and Donald Poffenberger, *The Sexual Trafficking in Children: An Investigation of the Child Sex Trade.* Dover, MA: Auburn House, 1988.

Child Sexual Exploitation: Improving Investigations and Protecting Victims—A Blueprint for Action, January 1995, http://www.ncjrs.org.

Eli Coleman, "The Development of Male Prostitution Activity Among Gay and Bisexual Adolescents," *Journal of Homosexuality* 17, no. 1–2, 1989.

Covenant House, *1995 Annual Report,* http://www.covenanthouse.org.

Anne Donnelly, "What We Have Learned About Prevention: What We Should Do About It," *Child Abuse and Neglect* 15, no. 1, 1991.

Dylan Foley, "AIDS Education for Teen Prostitutes," *Progressive,* February 1996.

J. Patrick Gannon, *Soul Survivors: A New Beginning for Adults Abused as Children.* New York: Prentice Hall, 1989.

Diana Gray, "Turning Out: A Study of Teenage Prostitution," *Urban Life and Culture,* January 1973.

J. L. Hazelton, "Runaways Find Trouble in Streets," *Akron Beacon Journal,* March 26, 1997.

Gerald T. Hotaling and David Finkelhor, *The Sexual Exploitation of Missing Children: A Research Review.* Washington, DC: Department of Justice, Office of Juvenile Justice and Delinquency Prevention, October 1988.

Robert P. McNamara, *The Times Square Hustler: Male Prostitution in New York City.* Westport, CT: Praeger, 1994.

J. Michael Murphy, Michael Jellinek et al., "Substance Abuse and Serious Child Mistreatment: Prevalence, Risk, and Outcome in a Court Sample," *Child Abuse and Neglect* 15, 1991.

Sonia Nazario, "Playing House: Troubled Teenagers Create a Fragile Family Beneath a Busy Street," *Wall Street Journal,* January 21, 1992.

Office of Juvenile Justice and Delinquency Prevention, *Child Abuse and Exploitation: Investigative Techniques.*

San Francisco Task Force on Prostitution, *Final Report 1996,* http://www.ci.sf.ca.us/reports/sftfp/1tf.htm.

Gitta Sereny, *The Invisible Children.* New York: Knopf, 1985.

Mimi H. Silbert and Ayala M. Pines, "Early Sexual Exploitation as an Influence in Prostitution," *Social Work,* July/August 1983.

Statistical Abstract of the United States 1995. Washington, DC: U.S. Department of Commerce, Bureau of the Census.

Arlene Stiffman, "Physical and Sexual Abuse in Runaway Youths," *Child Abuse and Neglect* 13, 1989.

Uniform Crime Reports for the United States 1995. Washington, DC: Federal Bureau of Investigation, U.S. Department of Justice.

D. Kelly Weisberg, *Children of the Night: A Study of Adolescent Prostitution.* Lexington, MA: Lexington Books, 1985.

Cathy Spatz Widom, "Childhood Sexual Abuse and Its Criminal Consequences," *Society,* May/June 1996.

Index

About the Authors

Ruth Dean is the president of the Writing Toolbox in Akron, Ohio. She writes books and articles and does research projects for health care organizations. She has taught English composition and research writing at the University of Akron and worked as a tutor in its Writing Center.

Melissa Thomson has a doctorate from Trinity College, Dublin, and taught seventh grade before moving to the United States. She writes articles and reports for the Writing Toolbox and sings in Apollo's Fire, a music group in Cleveland, Ohio.

Picture Credits